D0915974

TWENTIETH-CENTURY ENGLISH POETRY

An Introduction

TWENTIETH-CENTURY ENGLISH POETRY

An Introduction

by
ANTHONY THWAITE

HEINEMANN
LONDON

BARNES & NOBLE
NEW YORK

Heinemann Educational Books Ltd
LONDON EDINBURGH MELBOURNE AUCKLAND
TORONTO HONG KONG SINGAPORE
KUALA LUMPUR IBADAN NAIROBI
JOHANNESBURG LUSAKA NEW DELHI KINGSTON

U.K. edition
ISBN 0 435 18886 0 (cased)
    0 435 18887 9 (paper)

U.S. edition
ISBN 0 06 496890 1

Published in Great Britain by
Heinemann Educational Books Ltd
48 Charles Street, London W1X 8AH
Published in the U.S.A.
1978 by Harper & Row Publishers, Inc.
Barnes & Noble Import Division
Printed in Great Britain by
Richard Clay (The Chaucer Press), Ltd., Bungay, Suffolk

Contents

Acknowledgements

The author and publishers wish to thank the following for permission to reproduce copyright material:

Faber & Faber Ltd for lines from 'Elegy on Spain' from *Collected Poems 1935–55* by George Barker, extracts from *Collected Poems* by Edwin Muir, lines from 'Personal Helicon' from *Death of a Naturalist*, lines from 'Orange Drums, Tyrone 1966' and 'Bone Dreams' from *North* by Seamus Heaney, lines from 'Snow', 'Memoranda to Horace' and 'Apple Blossom' all from *The Collected Poems* by Louis MacNeice, extracts from *The Whitsun Weddings* and from *High Windows* by Philip Larkin, lines from 'The Thought Fox' from *Hawk in the Rain*, lines from 'Pibroch' from *Wodwo*, lines from 'Hawk Roosting' from *Lupercal* and 'A Childish Prank' from *Crow*, all by Ted Hughes, extracts from *Collected Poems* and *Journey to a War* by W. H. Auden, lines from 'The Waste Land' and 'Four Quartets' by T. S. Eliot, extracts from *Collected Poems* by Stephen Spender; Oxford University Press for *Death of a Naturalist* and *North* both by Seamus Heaney, extracts from *Collected Poems* by Edwin Muir, extracts from *The Collected Poems of Louis MacNeice* ed. by E. R. Dodds, extracts from *Collected Poems* by Stevie Smith; Random House Inc. for lines from 'The Still Centre' from *Ruins and Visions*, lines from 'Ultima Ratio Regum' from *Selected Poems*, lines from 'Two Armies' from *Collected Poems 1928–1953*, all by Stephen Spender, lines from 'Consider', 'Missing', 'In Time of War', 'Commentary', 'The Cave of Making', 'In Memory of W. B. Yeats, and III of 'Five Songs', all from *Collected Poems* by W. H. Auden, ed. by Edward Mendelson; Miss Anne Yeats and Macmillan Co. Ltd and A. P. Watt for extracts from *Collected Poems of W. B. Yeats*, A. P. Watt for extracts from *Collected Poems* by Robert Graves; Andre Deutsch Ltd for extracts from *Mercian Hymns* and *King Log* by Geoffrey Hill, extracts from *New Poems* by Roy Fuller, Andre Deutsch Ltd and Oxford University Press for extracts from *Collected Poems* by David Gascoyne; Jonathan Cape and the Executors of the Estate of C. Day Lewis for lines from 'The Unwanted' from *Collected Poems*, 'Walking Away' from *The Gate*, lines from the 'The House Where I Was Born' from *The Whispering Roots*, all by C. Day Lewis; Chatto and Windus Ltd for lines from 'Ignorance of Death' from *Collected Poems* by William Empson, extracts from *Collected Poems* by Wilfred Owen; J. M. Dent & Sons and the Trustees for the Copyrights of the late Dylan Thomas for extracts from *Collected Poems* by Dylan Thomas; Houghton Mifflin and Co. and John Murray (Publishers) Ltd for lines from 'NW5' from *Collected Poems* by John Betjeman; Martin Secker

Author's Note

This book has had a long and rather curious history. The very first version of it was published in 1957 by Kenkyusha Ltd, Tokyo, under the title *Essays on Contemporary English Poetry*. It was based on lectures I had given to students of English Literature at Tokyo University and elsewhere in Japan between 1955 and early 1957, specifically as a critical guide for a Japanese student audience. Largely on the strength of an appreciative review by G. S. Fraser in the *Times Literary Supplement*, I think, Jonathan Price (at that time working for Heinemann) persuaded his firm that it would be a good idea to commission a revised version for an English-speaking audience—the sixth form, college of education, university and 'general' reader. This (now called *Contemporary English Poetry: An Introduction*) appeared from Heinemann in 1959, and had further revised editions in 1961 and 1964, being last reprinted in 1968.

The book has been widely used, and over the years I have been both pleased and embarrassed at the way in which remarks from it have appeared in likely and unlikely places, from Poland to Pakistan: embarrassed, because my ideas and my style have inevitably altered, and I hope deepened and matured, over a period of twenty-odd years. When the last reprint was finally exhausted, I welcomed the invitation from Antony Beal of Heinemann Educational to make a much more thorough revision and expansion than hitherto. The present book is the result.

Its change of title to *Twentieth-Century English Poetry* reflects a change of attitude to the material. 'Contemporary,' as I say at the beginning of Chapter One, is 'a vaguely convenient device'. 'Twentieth-century' is both explicit and neutral. As for continuing to include Gerard Manley Hopkins, there is not only the 'modernity' of his poems but the fact that they were not properly available until 1918.

Anyone who bothers to compare earlier versions with this one will quickly see the changes: some of them comparatively small, as in the chapter on Hopkins, but most of them very extensive. At many points I use bits of material from other writings of mine: e.g., my survey commissioned by the British Council and published by Longman, *Poetry Today 1960–1973*, articles and reviews written for the *Times Literary Supplement*, *New Statesman*, *Encounter*, etc. and other, more fugitive places. I have benefited a great deal from various spells of teaching between 1965 and today in universities in Libya, Kuwait, Pakistan and elsewhere, from seminar teaching at the University of East Anglia, and from a good many extra-mural and extension classes in Britain.

In a generous review of the 1959 version, Frank Kermode said that it might have been a good idea to include some treatment of American poetry and 'thus dispel a slight air of parochialism'. The point would no doubt be even more strongly put today; but aware though I am of actions and interactions (as I hope Chapter One makes plain), I have been determined to keep the book to a manageable length. So the Americans are out, for reasons of space and not parochialism or chauvinism.

ANTHONY THWAITE
February 1977

Tharston,
Norfolk.

CHAPTER ONE

The Background of Contemporary Poetry

The label 'contemporary', or 'modern', is usually no more than a vaguely convenient device; like 'Romantic' or 'Classic', the words suggest something without defining it. Literary periods, like archaeological or historical periods, have been—and continue to be—invented, in a sense, as part of a basic human need to impose order on undifferentiated places, people, art-works, ideas. Some of the ordering we do is chronological: we know that Dryden lived and worked before Wordsworth—or if we don't, we had better take note of the fact. Sometimes we relate style to chronology: an archaeologist can distinguish between an Early Bronze Age pot and a Middle Bronze Age one without using Carbon-14 tests, and a sensitive and informed reader can distinguish between an anonymous passage from a seventeenth-century poet and one from a nineteenth-century poet—though there are of course no literary Carbon-14 tests with which he can back up his judgement. Often we work with hindsight; we know, or think we know, what and when the Middle Ages were —but we must be aware of all those people who lived through the Middle Ages without knowing that they *were* the Middle Ages.

These remarks of mine are not whimsical preliminaries, but suggestions about how much more difficult it is to make sense of 'movements' and 'developments' in our own time; difficult for the political or social historian as well as for the commentator on or critic of the arts. The work of the first poet I consider in detail in this book, Gerard Manley Hopkins, was published well within the lifetime of many people still living; yet he was wholly 'a Victorian', as far as his own lifespan goes, and in some ways a conventional Victorian. But does it make any difference if we think (as F. R. Leavis does) of Hopkins as the greatest poet of the Victorian age, or as an 'early modern'? How much do we play with time, manipulate it, to make patterns that satisfy us?

That there was something, now past and to be seen as a historical phenomenon, which can identifiably be called 'the modernist movement' or 'modernism' is accepted doctrine among many academic literary folk today. Not that all of them mean the same thing when they use such terms: some people would see Hopkins as involved in 'modernism', others would not see any such movement as beginning until perhaps twenty years after Hopkins's death. This chapter aims to touch on and expand such points, relating them to actual poets, actual poems.

1900, the beginning of the century, might be seen as a convenient and nicely rounded date at which to begin. In the introduction he wrote to his *Oxford Book of Modern Verse* in 1936, W. B. Yeats, after drawing on his memories of the London poets of the 1890s, put it this way:

> Then in 1900 everybody got down off his stilts; henceforth nobody drank absinthe with his black coffee; nobody went mad; nobody committed suicide; nobody joined the Catholic church; or if they did I have forgotten.
>
> Victorianism had been defeated . . .

Of course Yeats is being facetious: the extravagant life-styles of such poets as Ernest Dowson and Lionel Johnson are gently mocked by a man who had been their contemporary but who had long outlived them. 1900 marks nothing but the beginning of a century. The 'establishment' poets were Alfred Austin (the Poet Laureate who had been appointed after Tennyson's death), Robert Bridges (Austin's successor), Henry Newbolt, Alfred Noyes, William Watson—the last of whom is praised in that same anthology introduction for his 'noble eloquence'. Kipling was active and popular, in both prose and verse. Swinburne, though for long in a state of mental and physical decline, was thought by many good judges to be the best living poet. Stephen Phillips, the verse playwright, was seen by some as a splendidly Shakespearian poet. In this same year, T. E. Brown's collected poems were published—a book that survives on the strength of two lines:

> A garden is a lovesome thing,
> God wot!

W. E. Henley (of whom Yeats said that he 'had turned the young men at Oxford and Cambridge into imperialists') published his book of poems *For England's Sake*. Yeats's own verse drama, *The Shadowy Waters*, appeared. Oscar Wilde died, in exile after his release from prison.

It was not a revolutionary moment, nor a period of complete stagnation. Hardy, who was sixty in 1900, was in full production as a poet, pushed back to poetry after the furore over *Jude the Obscure* in 1895. A. E. Housman, in his proud and bitter isolation, had brought out *A Shropshire Lad* in 1896 in a private edition, and the South African War soon afterwards made very popular its mixture of patriotic pride and stoical gloom, pessimism and nostalgia:

> East and west on fields forgotten
> Bleach the bones of comrades slain,
> Lovely lads and dead and rotten;
> None that go return again.

Hardy's and Housman's poems are still with us, undiminished; but no one could call them 'modern'. Whatever was 'modern' was, in 1900, stirring fitfully in the wings; perhaps through Arthur Symons's awareness of what was happening in Paris— and Symons was Yeats's friend; he was also the author of *The Symbolist Movement in Literature* (1899), a book that was instrumental in bringing to the attention of the young T. S. Eliot the poetry of Jules Laforgue. In a quite different way, Walt Whitman (who had died in America in 1892, the same year as Tennyson) was beginning to be a powerful influence not only in his own country but in Britain and Europe; even in the 1880s, both Hopkins and Yeats had been strongly moved by him—and Whitman was notoriously new and shocking, even though his *Leaves of Grass* had first been published as long ago as 1855.

In fact 'modern' English poetry has often been seen to have its origins in France and America. In his book *A Map of Modern English Verse*, John Press makes an interesting case for saying that 'the years 1908 to 1910 have a good claim to be regarded as a crucial phase in the history of English poetry', by linking together Ezra Pound's arrival in London, Ford Madox Ford's founding of the *English Review*, Eliot's reading of *The Symbolist Movement in Literature*, the first Post-Impressionist Exhibition in London and the visit of Diaghilev's Russian Ballet—'modernism' in literature, painting and music seen as a common force. By the beginning of the First World War in 1914, a number of movements can be seen at work, whether in essence or in embryo: Futurism, Vorticism, Imagism. In the American magazine *Poetry*, for which Ezra Pound wrote notes and commentaries about what was going on in England, he asserted in the January 1913 issue: 'The youngest school here that has the nerve to call itself a school is that of the *Imagistes*.' Ambivalent and critical though Pound was about the self-styled members of this 'school', he himself is probably the best exemplar of their notions and methods: 'to use the language of common speech, but to employ always the *exact* word, not the nearly-exact, nor the merely decorative word . . . To create new rhythms—as the expression of new moods—and not to copy old rhythms, which merely echo old moods . . . To produce poetry that is hard and clear, never blurred nor indefinite.' And here is Pound's complete poem 'In a Station of the Metro':

> The apparition of these faces in the crowd;
> Petals on a wet, black bough.

If the Imagist aim was towards compression, hardness, clarity, these were congenial aims for Pound as well; but the actual practice of Imagism, in the poems of such writers as Amy Lowell, H. D. (Hilda Doolittle) and Richard Aldington, was unimpressive. Pound was more restless, wider ranging, quickly drawing into his ambit both Yeats and Eliot, and having a profound effect on what they wrote. 'Experiment' was consciously, sometimes truculently, in the air from at least as early as Pound's

Poetry note in 1913 right through the 1920s. There were other areas of literary revolt: the anthology *Wheels*, for example, which was mainly a platform for the Sitwell family. And in 1923 —the year after Eliot published *The Waste Land*—there was almost a riot at the Aeolian Hall in London, where Edith Sitwell first read her poem sequence *Façade* through a megaphone concealed behind a giant mask-backcloth, to the accompaniment of William Walton's music. No doubt it was ploys such as this that caused F. R. Leavis to utter his famous pronouncement that 'the Sitwells belong to the history of publicity rather than of poetry'.

One must remember that there was a continuing current of objection to all such experiment—objection which hardly cared to make distinctions between, say, *The Waste Land* and the Aeolian Hall *Façade*, or between the trio of jocularly named 'Steins'—'Ep, Ein, and Gertrude'. This counter-current can be seen in the anthologies of *Georgian Poetry*, edited by Sir Edward Marsh and issued between 1912 and 1920; in the work of G. K. Chesterton, John Drinkwater, John Masefield, J. C. Squire, Humbert Wolfe; and in the anthologies for schools edited by Squire. To the poetry-reading public of the First World War and the 1920s (and in many cases even later), this was modern poetry, these were the modern poets. The blurring of the scene, however, is suggested by the fact that both Robert Graves and D. H. Lawrence appeared in some volumes of *Georgian Poetry*, and that Wilfred Owen (the year before his death) was apparently proud to write that 'I am held peer by the Georgians; I am a poet's poet'. 'Georgian' can too readily be used as an automatic sneer.

The earlier volumes of *Georgian Poetry* sold very well, so well that it took Marsh and many others by surprise. There seemed to be a public for poetry—and this has been one of the continuing swings of the pendulum in the modern period: between moments when poetry has suddenly seemed to catch the public mood, and moments when it has seemed to be talking only to itself. The audience for poetry has unquestionably diminished since, say, the time when a new book by Tennyson would be eagerly awaited by a large non-specialist public and would go into many editions. Yet alongside the shrinking of this 'general' public there has grown up an educational one—all those who, because of syllabus requirements at school, college or university, are required to read Hopkins, Yeats, Eliot, Owen, or one anthology or another of 'contemporary verse'. The effects of this are of course mixed. For some people, as soon as a writer is 'set' in this pedagogic sense, he is doomed. It is a sad irony that, as a student audience for poetry has grown, a lay audience has shrunk—though there have been, and are, a number of exceptions, of whom John Betjeman is probably the obvious recent example. (I am not talking in terms of such popular figures as Patience Strong—who reputedly sells quarter of a million copies of her verses each year in South Africa alone—or the meteoric success in the 1970s of Pam Ayres. One has to draw the line somewhere.)

The 'difficulty' of modern poetry is perhaps less harped on today than it was thirty or forty years ago; partly because the most widely admired poets now writing, such as Philip Larkin and Ted Hughes, are—whatever their considerable differences—hardly ever 'obscure' in the way that Eliot, say, was considered so in the 1920s. In any case, one should have a sense of perspective about the battles new poetry has to fight over charges of difficulty. An extract from Hazlitt's 1816 review of Coleridge's 'Kubla Khan' may implicitly bear out what I mean:

> Upon the whole, we look upon this publication as one of the most notable pieces of impertinence of which the press has lately been made guilty; and one of the boldest experiments that has yet been made on the patience or understanding of the public. The thing now before us is utterly destitute of value. It exhibits from beginning to end not a ray of genius . . . raving . . . drivelling . . . nonsense.

A deeper question than that of 'difficulty' concerns in what ways modern English poets have either influenced or reflected the time in which they live. Shelley's view of poets as 'the unacknowledged legislators of the world', for all its familiarity, probably rings a hollow note nowadays. At the very time Shelley was writing, poets were more and more becoming seen as isolated figures—sometimes heroic or noble perhaps, sometimes dangerously exciting (like Byron, and Shelley himself), but also remote from 'the world'. These feelings, which are Romantic ones, still persist. After all, we still live in an atmosphere which has had many of its attitudes to the arts determined by the Romantic Movement. And Romanticism in itself encourages heterodoxy, diversity, individuality. More and more, reading the literature of the twentieth century, one has a sense of individuals looking for individual forms of expression; and this is reflected in criticism, in the recurring words of evaluation and comment— 'original', 'disturbing', 'a new voice', 'finding his own voice', 'developing', 'individual' itself. Such terms, and the concepts behind them, would have been puzzling or even incomprehensible to a pre-Coleridge or pre-Shelley world.

In some moments of apparent crisis, the modern poet has 'warned'—in the sense that Wilfred Owen and W. H. Auden warned; but not from a position of political centrality, as Milton and Marvell spoke from positions, however precarious, of being in the middle of events; or as Pope or Tennyson did, as men on intimate terms with those in political power. Two world wars, the extension of totalitarianism on a vast scale, the simultaneous releases and tensions brought about by Freud and post-Freudian psychology, the bewildering proliferations of science and technology—all these have played their part in both stimulating and isolating the poet. To put it deliberately crassly, it is no longer easy to be simple; and it is almost impossible for the poet to have either the self-confidence or the desire to lead, legislate, or prescribe. He is seen in terms partly moral or didactic ('What does he say?'), but much more in aesthetic terms ('How does he say it?', 'What sort of object is this poem?') and as someone who is 'expressing himself' ('What sort of person has written this poem?', 'What sort of experience is he communicating?'). Most of the tenets of modern response and modern literary criticism, however subtly or opaquely they may be put, seem to reduce themselves to these questions.

There remain the traditional, inherited frames and calipers with which we try to enclose and examine poets and poems: literary history, biography, 'background' . . . In the original version of this book, I ended the introductory chapter with some remarks which—though I now see them as naively expressed—are still as close as I can get to the matter: '. . . a poem is in some sense a reflection of the life it comes from; it cannot be disengaged from life, treated in isolation as a piece of artistic mechanism. "If poetry comes not as naturally as the leaves to a tree," wrote Keats, "it had better not come at all." And the reading of poetry should be as natural as that, too—though that does not mean we should not sometimes find ourselves puzzled by a poem, so that we have to tease out the meaning by taking thought. The reader must sometimes be prepared to work almost as hard while he reads as the poet did while he wrote. Even the tree, in its instinctive way, puts a good deal of effort into making those leaves.' The injunction is: now read on.

CHAPTER TWO

Gerard Manley Hopkins (1844–1889)

When Robert Bridges in 1918 (twenty-nine years after Hopkins's death) brought out the first edition of *The Poems of Gerard Manley Hopkins*, he wrote a prefatory sonnet to the book, the last two lines of which address the poet in this way:

> Go forth: amidst our chaffinch flock display
> Thy plumage of far wonder and heavenward flight!

But this was prophecy rather than immediate fact; the 'chaffinch flock' of 1918 was not much better prepared for Hopkins than was the Victorian world in which he died—indeed, the literary world of 1918 was still in many ways one that had inherited the precept and practice of the Victorians. It was not until a second edition appeared in 1930 (this time edited by Charles Williams) that Hopkins began to enjoy the reputation which has now raised him to the level of a major poet, or something very like one.

The forty-year neglect of Hopkins's poetry can be explained simply by referring to Bridges' introduction to the first edition, in which he seems to be a great deal on the defensive, acknowledging freely what he calls 'Oddity' and 'Obscurity', 'faults of taste' and 'blemishes in the poet's style'. Even the *Times Literary Supplement*, which in 1919 gave the book what must have seemed an astonishingly appreciative review, did not question these criticisms by Bridges; and though the review ends with the remark that the poems are 'authentic fragments that we trust even when they bewilder us', this is a fair example of its severe reservations:

> His worst trick is that of passing from one word to another . . .
> merely because they are alike in sound. This, at its worst, produces
> the effect almost of idiocy, of speech without sense and prolonged
> merely by echoes. It seems to be a bad habit, like stuttering, except
> that he did not strive against it.

This irritation with Hopkins's style, as if at best it was showy mannerism and at worst a self-indulgent 'bad habit', is typical of early responses to his poetry. The fact that Bridges printed Hopkins's own 'Author's Preface' at the beginning of the first edition is partly to blame. One must not think of this guide to his own metrical rules as being like an apologia or manifesto (such as Wordsworth's preface to the *Lyrical Ballads*) addressed to the public, but as a private synopsis from one practitioner to another about technical matters. It is wrong to approach Hopkins's poetry by way of his own specialized nomenclature—Sprung Rhythm, Falling Feet, Outrides, Counterpoint Rhythm and so on; not that one can ignore the technique (it is hardly there to be ignored), but a more primary question is why he came to acquire it.

The striking quality of Hopkins's poetry lies in its energy. The poems grapple with their themes rather than comment on them; they act rather than react; and this is in contrast with a kind of poetry for which Hopkins invented a name. In a letter, written when he was only twenty, to an Oxford friend, he discussed what he called *Parnassian* poetry—poetry written on the slopes or levels of a poet's ability, not at the peak:

> It can only be spoken by poets, but is not in the highest sense poetry. It does not require the mood of mind in which the poetry of inspiration is written. It is spoken *on and from the level* of a poet's mind, not . . . when the inspiration, which is the gift of genius, raises him above himself.

And he goes on to say how most poets, great and small, sooner or later develop their own brand of Parnassian, their own habitual way of saying things. But to Hopkins, working in almost complete isolation, verse-writing was never a professional habit but a continually changing struggle with new material. His poetic energy came from two sources: first, from his close observation of, and excitement about, the natural world, in its most detailed and particularized forms; second, from the great stress caused not only by the violent, exultant effect of nature on him, but also by the clash in his personality of the sensuous man and artist he naturally was and the ascetic Jesuit he had chosen to become. Very broadly, one can say that the first resulted in his excited,

exuberant 'nature' poetry, emphasizing the grandeur and glory
of God; and the second in the dark, personal poems of spiritual
combat.

Nature (that is, all created things, including man) was to
Hopkins what the Sacraments are to Christians: 'an outward and
visible sign of an inward and spiritual grace'. Only man can see
these signs and understand their meaning, can glorify God for the
meaning behind the appearance and for the appearance itself:

> And what is Earth's eye, tongue, or heart else, where
> Else, but in dear and dogged man?

And nature reveals itself, not simply in one way, but in a variety
which in every created object is different. This difference, this
individual distinction, Hopkins called *inscape*; and the energy
which determines that individuality, and which keeps it distinct,
he called *instress*. He coined these two terms, just as he coined
Parnassian, because a new concept demands a new word; and
Hopkins's mind (controlled though it was by his self-imposed
religious discipline, and schooled in humility) was startlingly
original. Geoffrey Grigson has called Hopkins's poetry 'a passionate science'. It is a good phrase, for Hopkins observed and
recorded with all the scrupulous exactness of a scientist as well as
with the passionate excitement of an artist. His journals, written
from 1866–75, show how minute and exact his apprehension
was; everything, from the way a waterfall breaks up on the rocks
below to the sensation of drawing one's hand through a cluster
of damp bluebells, from the sequence of shapes into which a
cloudbank breaks in the sky to the ooze which comes from the
nostrils of a dying sheep, is caught and preserved. The observa-
tions, as they exist in the journals, are perhaps closer to the
scientist than to the poet; but they sparked into poetry.

One year in particular—1877—was rich in poems which
sprang from this observing and glorifying impulse: in that year
he wrote 'God's Grandeur', 'The Starlight Night', 'Spring', 'The
Sea and the Skylark', 'The Windhover', 'Pied Beauty' and
'Hurrahing in Harvest'. These, I feel, are the poems to which a
reader unacquainted with Hopkins should first come, because

they communicate most immediately the excitement, the individuality, the *instress* itself of his poetry. Hopkins himself thought 'The Windhover' 'the best thing I ever wrote'. But before looking at what he considered his masterpiece, it might be better to read a poem which, equally implicitly but more simply, gives one a clear picture of Hopkins's excitement about instress and inscape: 'Pied Beauty'.

It is a poem of praise to God for the variousness of his creation; the beauty of the world, Hopkins says, is 'pied'—that is, variegated and parti-coloured, dappled and subtle. His method in the poem is to list things which change from moment to moment, from season to season; things whose function, appearance, characteristics, mark them out separately and individually—the changing patterns of the sky, like the 'brinded' (brindled, dappled) hide of a cow; the small pink or red moles which lie, like the points of stippled paint from an artist's brush, on a trout's back; the contrast between the rich red-brown nut of the fallen ripe chestnut and the green husk or case which encloses it, a contrast which he likens to the glowing flame which is revealed by breaking open a lit coal; the varied browns and yellows of finches' wings; the patchwork of landscapes, changing, according to time and place, from the green of the fold where the animals are pastured to the dull fawn-brown of land left fallow and the rich deep brown of fields newly ploughed; and then all the specialist 'gear and tackle and trim' of men's different jobs.

Then, moving from particulars, he lists more generally the contrasts and antitheses of life which create inscape and instress—all things set in opposition, all things new or which strike one with a shock of newness, all things whose function is individual and economical ('spare'). All these things whose nature is 'freckled' with opposites in union are products of God, who 'fathers-forth' (analogous to 'bringing forth' a child). Yet God himself is 'past' (or 'above') change; he who creates is not the same as his creations; they are *signs* of his powers of invention, of individuation. These things 'praise him'; but the final words of the poem are really an imperative, addressed to man—'Praise him—it is your duty, and should be your delight as well, to do so'.

If 'Pied Beauty' uses a cataloguing method to suggest the splendour and variety of creation, 'The Windhover' concentrates on a single example, a kestrel. The moment of excitement in watching (and in a sense becoming part of) this primal creature is 'caught'; the poem is an act of exalted capture. The opening lines see the bird gliding, hovering, swooping and returning, and the movement is imitated in the movement of the lines: the alliteration, the internal and line-end rhymes, the exclamatory sweeps and rushes of the syntax, work together to achieve this, and are themselves a 'mastery'. The bird is a prince, a knight, a horseman, a ringing bell, a skate sweeping effortlessly on the ice; it is also a showing-forth in miniature of 'Christ our Lord', to whom the poem is dedicated and to whom Hopkins speaks directly from the moment of the strong break at 'AND the fire that breaks from thee then . . .' The poet's heart has been 'in hiding', subdued. Now it finds power and meaning even in drudgery, just as the ploughshare, guided down the furrow ('sillion'), is polished by the movement of the earth against it; and inside the dull embers is a glowing heart of fire. The heart is renewed, strengthened, made beautiful, by the superb mastery of the windhover.

A poem which puts Hopkins's ideas of 'selfhood' (essential individual quality) more generally and philosophically is 'As kingfishers catch fire, dragonflies draw flame', written four or five years after the important 1877 poems. Everything, Hopkins says, has its own characteristics, through which it expresses its 'selfhood' and the purpose for which it was made:

> Each mortal thing does one thing and the same:
> Deals out that being indoors each one dwells;
> Selves—goes itself; *myself* it speaks and spells,
> Crying *What I do is me: for that I came.*

But, more importantly—because man is seen as God's highest creation on earth—man is the chief medium through whom God acts and reveals himself:

> I say more: the just man justices;
> Keeps grace: that keeps all his goings graces;

Acts in God's eye what in God's eye he is—
Christ—for Christ plays in ten thousand places,
Lovely in limbs, and lovely in eyes not his
To the Father through the features of men's faces.

In some words from a sermon which Hopkins, as Jesuit priest, delivered, 'Man was created to praise'.

This was Hopkins the passionate observer, excited by observation of nature and of man into an exultant poetic energy. But there was also the Hopkins who experienced agonizing spiritual desolation, who bowed his will to the discipline of the order he had chosen, who struggled always to do his best as parish priest, as teacher, as man of God, yet who so often felt that he had failed. His clash of personality and will, aggravated by periodic bouts of ill-health, led him to depression and sometimes almost to despair. The resultant tensions are found in his so-called 'Terrible' sonnets of 1885—'Carrion Comfort', 'No worst, there is none', 'I wake and feel the fell of dark', 'Patience, hard thing!', 'My own heart let me have more pity on', and one or two others. There is energy here, too, but it is that of a spirit trying to struggle up from despair, not exuberance at the exciting rightness of creation.

W. H. Gardner has put very well the basis of these poems:

Desolation is the human shuddering recoil from the strain of a rigorous discipline—a sourness, loss of hope, of joy, almost a suspension of faith itself, which makes the victim feel that he is totally separated from God.

Yet, he continues,

underneath the despair and complaint the note of willing self-surrender to the higher necessity is always implicit ... [These poems] are the work of a man who, while putting the whole of his 'sad self' into a poem, could still preserve the sensitivity and control of the artist ...

The poem 'I wake and feel the fell of dark' begins with the impression of darkness and despair smothering light and hope. 'The fell of dark' blends and interlocks three senses—the weight and smothering effect of an animal's 'fell' or hairy skin; the archaic

adjective 'fell' used as a noun, to mean 'painfulness', 'ruthless-
ness', 'cruelty'; and the dialect noun 'fell' (from the verb 'to
fell'), meaning 'a knock-down blow'. The compound of these is
that he wakes and feels the heavy blow and cruel, crushing weight
of night—with all its fears and nightmares—rather than the clear,
kind light of day. His heart has been wandering through terrify-
ing, uncharted darkness for the unimaginably long hours of the
night, and is still condemned to it 'in yet longer light's delay'.
He knows through experience ('with witness') that he has suffered
and will continue to suffer this torture; in a great hyperbole of
despair, he says that he is not speaking simply in terms of hours,
of a short time, but of life. He calls constantly to God, but his
cries are like letters sent to a distant country, letters which never
arrive. God, indeed, seems to live very far away, and is so remote
that the poet, in his despondency, despairs of ever reaching him.

But the despair is, after all, part of the man himself; he sees it
as self-generated:

> I am gall, I am heartburn. God's most deep decree
> Bitter would have me taste: my taste was me;
> Bones built in me, flesh filled, blood brimmed the curse.

The 'selfyeast' of his spirit sours the 'dull dough' of his body;
Hopkins takes his analogy from the making of bread, in which
the yeast acts by itself and makes the dough rise. So it is his selfish
ego which makes his body, and hence his spirit, chafe and fret,
souring what should be his wholesomeness. Acknowledging this,
he turns to consider 'the lost'—those in Hell—whose spiritual
disease was close to his, and whose present state makes his own
plight seem small: in paraphrase, 'I realize that those in Hell are
in this condition, and that their torture—like mine—is that of
being isolated in the Hell of their own selves, and thus cut off
from God; but their torment—because it is absolute—is far worse
than mine.' The final implication is that there is still hope; and
that to be 'selved', 'inscaped' *absolutely* is the worst damnation.
Thus the individuation of the 'nature' poems is glorious because
it is in relation to God; but individuation without that relationship is spiritual death.

The emotional conflict which forced these poems into being is perhaps hard to come to terms with; in a largely secularized society, most readers will feel remote from spiritual desolation of such a specifically Christian kind. But there remains, in the finished product, in the poems, 'the sensitivity and control of the artist' to which W. H. Gardner drew attention. Hopkins was a serious and dedicated craftsman, with an attitude to poetry which —despite his humility, his putting his job as a priest far above his literary work—one must call professional. His journals and his letters to the handful of poets to whom he showed his work (Bridges, R. W. Dixon and Coventry Patmore) show that. And his technique, though it was based on much scholarly inquiry into Latin, Greek, Welsh and English (standard, archaic and dialect English) metrics and vocabulary, was not mere exercise-writing or elaborate invention in the void; it was formed and perfected because only in these metres, in these words, could he best say what he had to say. Yeats made a great mistake when he called Hopkins's manner 'a last development of poetic diction', for poetic diction—language at several elegant removes from life —was precisely what Hopkins avoided. In a letter to Bridges, he wrote:

> Poetical language should be the current language heightened, to any degree heightened and unlike itself, but not . . . an obsolete one. This is Shakespeare's and Milton's practice.

But, he added, 'passing freaks and graces are another thing'. Hopkins's poetry is written in a language of excitement; it is thus very much 'heightened' language, and the 'passing freaks and graces' add to the individual quality of the excitement. He used the full resources of the language and, when those resources seemed to be inadequate, he invented, or made new and surprising marriages. There are all the specialist words (such as 'sillion' in 'The Windhover'), dialect words (such as 'degged' in 'Inversnaid' and 'fashed' in 'The Leaden Echo and the Golden Echo'); compound words, the invention of a man whose mind enjoyed all the cognate and sound-linked flavours and shades of language: 'spendsavour salt', 'beadbonny ash', 'selfyeast of spirit', 'wanwood leafmeal', and with these all the intricate interplay of alliteration, internal rhyme, assonance, dissonance. Like Shakespeare, he forced language into his own mould, making words do service as new parts of speech—nouns become verbs, adjectives become adverbs; definite and indefinite articles and relative pronouns are omitted if they hold up the free flow of mind and rhythm.

As for his metrical technique, perhaps only one important thing needs to be said about Sprung Rhythm: that it reads, and scans, purely by stress and not by number of syllables. This means that language does not need to be forced on to a Procrustean bed of metre. Hopkins himself expressed it lucidly enough in a letter to Bridges:

> Why do I employ sprung rhythm at all? Because it is the nearest to the rhythm of prose, that is the native and natural rhythm of speech, the least forced, the most rhetorical and emphatic of all rhythms, combining, as it seems to me, opposite and, one would have thought, incompatible excellences, markedness of rhythm— that is rhythm's self—and naturalness of expression . . .

To get the full force of his rhythms, one should read 'The Wreck of the Deutschland' (the long poem with which he resumed his career as a poet in 1875, after a self-imposed silence of seven years) and his astonishing bravura performance 'The Leaden Echo and the Golden Echo'. Both poems are difficult at first, but in reading them one should take Hopkins's advice: 'take breath and read it with the ears, as I always wish to be read, and my verse becomes all right'. The energy in Hopkins's poetry has a truly physical quality; it becomes the thing it is about. Reading it requires a pleasurable and bracing physical effort, and the way into his work itself grows clearer.

As far as later poets are concerned, one can almost make it a rule that Hopkins cannot be learned from *directly*; he is in no ordinary sense a possible, or good, model; what shows through is the mannerism, not the mind, and Hopkins-influenced mannerisms can be found here and there in Auden, Day Lewis, Dylan

Thomas and George Barker. The uniqueness of his life, his vocation and his personality still isolate him as he was isolated in his lifetime. Unlike his contemporary, Hardy (who outlived him by almost forty years), Hopkins did not hand on a legacy which writers can use other than by imitating him. But the work survives in its own right, to be discovered and enjoyed.

CHAPTER THREE

W. B. Yeats (1865–1939)

Yeats is perhaps the supreme example in poetry of a man who willed himself into greatness. It was a greatness achieved through coming to terms with his own diversity. In one of his autobiographical writings, looking back on himself as a young man, he says that at that time a sentence seemed to form in his head, without conscious effort: 'Hammer your thoughts into unity.' For days, he says, he could think of nothing else, and for years he tested all he did by that sentence. Restlessly, self-consciously, self-questioningly, making leaps of imaginative connection that are sometimes hard to follow logically, he constructed his own poetic world slowly and painfully through a long lifetime of experience.

At the turn of the century, when he was thirty-five, he had a reasonably secure minor reputation as a poet who was delicate, melancholy, fond of dreamy and faery-like Irish themes. His book *The Wind Among the Reeds*, published in 1899, is indeed full of dreams, fairies, a profusion of such adjectives as 'dim', 'grey', 'pale' and such combinations as 'cloud-pale' and 'dream-dimmed'. The poems are soft, mellifluous, vague and disembodied. The Irish references (such as to 'Wandering Aengus') make Yeats distinct from his contemporaries and friends in London—Arthur Symons, Lionel Johnson, Ernest Dowson—but all these poets shared a plangent insubstantial quality. Johnson and Dowson died young, Symons lived on but became repetitious and then, for the last decades of his life, silent. Yeats outgrew them, discovering new themes, new modes, new selves: not 'a unity', but a succession of unities, of selves.

Yeats's father, John Butler Yeats, though sympathetic to his son's literary ambitions, was a rationalist, a sceptic, someone who had consciously rebelled against the Christian pieties of his own childhood. J. B. Yeats thought his son's preoccupations with the occult and with Irish nationalist politics foolishly distracting, and there is much in W.B.'s autobiographical writing and theorizing to make one sympathize with the father's view. There can seldom have been a poet who was more unerringly drawn towards dubious, absurd or even bogus notions. But Yeats's toughness of spirit, integrity of purpose, and—most of all—the gradual sharpening of his own verbal and rhythmical technique, brought into being a body of work which shakes itself free from the enthusiasms that inspired it or fed it.

Not that one can quite ignore those enthusiasms: an ignorant reading of Yeats is as bad as one that occupies itself with too reverent or elaborate delving into pernes, gyres, cycles of the moon, and all the other paraphernalia that for years Yeats needed as a quasi-rationalization of what he was doing. As with Blake (with whom at one stage Yeats identified himself, as mage and seer), it is not always a commonsensical matter of 'Never trust the singer, trust the song'. The new colloquial tone one begins to see with the publication of his volume *The Green Helmet* in 1910 is partly there because of his political nationalist enthusiasms—an accordance with 'The book of the people'; it becomes more obvious in *Responsibilities* (1914), and turns into a wholly individual voice in *Michael Robartes and the Dancer* (1921). And along with this, yet conversely, goes an equally strong desire to codify the mystical map of history—an effort that resulted in that obscure, often maddening but necessary book, *A Vision* (1925). One cannot explain away the Irishman and the visionary.

Speaking of his own Irish generation of poets—Synge, Gogarty, George Russell—he wrote (in 'Coole Park and Ballylee'):

> We were the last romantics—chose for theme
> Traditional sanctity and loveliness;
> Whatever's written in what poets name
> The book of the people; whatever most can bless
> The mind of man or elevate a rhyme.

It is self-dramatizing and also self-historicizing; to see something-or-other as 'the last' is a job for the future, not for the present. It is a pose, one of the very many that Yeats adopted during his life, one of the masks which he put on and through which he spoke. But until one sees the necessity of these masks and poses to Yeats, there will be small returns in the poetry, except in terms of acknowledging the development of an (apparently) more direct technical attack as time went on. To range himself alongside 'traditional sanctity and loveliness' was not just to subscribe to 'the romantics'; it was to lament an order that was passing—the great houses and the aristocracy that lived in them, a sense of nobility, of reverence, of order, in a society that was stratified into unity. He was no egalitarian; one remembers his unpleasant sneer, 'base-born products of base beds'. But the lament is for lost roots, lost coherence. Again and again the contrast between rootlessness and a sense of place, between elegance (which need not be aristocratic) and formlessness, is treated in Yeats's work. Elsewhere in 'Coole Park and Ballylee':

> Where fashion or mere fantasy decrees
> We shift about—all that great glory spent—
> Like some poor Arab tribesman and his tent.

The theme is worked through less abstractly, more humanely, in 'A Prayer for my Daughter'. Yeats's marriage in 1917 brought him not only the unexpected gift of his wife's automatic writing, which supplied him with images, but a vantage-point of stability; the birth of his children gave him an actual stake in the future. With this seems to come a new maturity. The human qualities he encapsulates in 'A Prayer for my Daughter' are significant. He wishes her beauty—though he importantly qualifies this, tempering it with thoughts of Maud Gonne, with whose great beauty, intellect and passion he had fallen in love more than quarter of a century earlier, whom he had lost, and whom he saw become a political demagogue, an arouser of political hatred. He wishes the child courtesy; roots in 'one dear perpetual place'; lack of hatred; self-reliance; and—most important of all—a life based on 'ceremony' and 'custom', two words which are pivots on which the whole poem turns:

> Ceremony's a name for the rich horn,
> And custom for the spreading laurel tree.

By 'the rich horn' Yeats means the Horn of Plenty, the cornucopia, the gifts with which a fortunate child is born; a birthright he has already referred to in the fourth and eighth stanzas of the poem. In particular, he means by 'ceremony' the gift of living one's life with a cool and unruffled elegance, as a ritual. As for the laurel, it is brought into the sixth stanza as a symbol of rooted-ness; he prays that his daughter may

> live like some green laurel
> Rooted in one dear perpetual place.

In other words, may she have that sense of belonging which, until his marriage late in middle age, Yeats himself had never possessed.

Yeats, indeed, was rootless and restless for much of his life: a Protestant (and on his father's side actually of English descent) in a largely Catholic country, an Irishman for part of his childhood and young manhood in London. From his early days, he was steeped in Irish mythology and folk-lore, and found emotional nourishment in these, but in his early poems the use he made of the tales and legends was fanciful and decorative. Towards the end of his life, he dismissed them contemptuously as

> Themes . . . that might adorn old songs or courtly shows.

Even when his themes were not of Cathleen ni Houlihan, Wandering Aengus, Oisin and other misty figures of Celtic legend, the world of his early poems was one of daydreams—as in one of his most famous poems, 'The Lake Isle of Innisfree' (from *The Rose*, 1893). Despite the seeming particularity of the 'nine bean-rows' and the 'hive for the honey-bee', the country retreat he yearningly presents is—in the manner of daydreams—only vaguely present. This womb-like Ireland was something Yeats consciously rejected in later years; in his 'The Municipal Gallery Revisited' (from *Last Poems*, 1939) he accepted, though apprehensively, a new Ireland:

> This is not
> The dead Ireland of my youth, but an Ireland
> The poets have imagined, terrible and gay.

Reality forced this change in his attitude. During the First World War, while Britain was preoccupied and almost all its troops involved in France and Belgium, southern Ireland rebelled, and later proclaimed itself a republic. Fierce fighting broke out in 1916 (the Easter Rising), and continued sporadically until 1922, with the whole island involved in civil war, and with much brutality on the part of both the Irish and the English. It was a bitter struggle, of which we still have the legacy in Ulster, and behind it lay the whole sad history of the Irish people: the Elizabethan ravages, the repression and forced settlements under Cromwell, the hunger for land and for food, the fanaticism of battling factions and ideologies. As Yeats put it in 'Remorse for Intemperate Speech' (1931):

> Out of Ireland have we come.
> Great hatred, little room,
> Maimed us at the start.
> I carry from my mother's womb
> A fanatic heart.

Yeats was ambivalent in his attitude towards this hatred and violence. It was part of a struggle for the independence of his native country, at times it seemed glorified as something through which men struggled towards greatness and nobility, yet it was also something which soured and destroyed men; and the violence then was not an expression of patriotism but merely that of 'weasels fighting in a hole'. Sometimes he was stricken with remorse because he thought that he himself, as a known supporter of and propagandist for Irish nationalism, might have been partly responsible:

> Come fix upon me that accusing eye,
> I thirst for accusation. All that was said,
> All that was sung in Ireland is a lie
> Bred out of the contagion of the throng.

Or, more starkly, his direct questioning of guilt:

> Did that play of mine send out
> Certain men the English shot . . . ?
> Could my spoken words have checked
> That whereby a house lay wrecked?

He looked for heroism, but too often found instead a meanness of spirit, a selfishness and a crude materialism in the Irish political leaders and journalists—and in the Irish 'mob'—which seemed to Yeats to have poisoned the great-heartedness of the legendary Irish nobility. He found a more recent symbol of the old heroism in O'Leary, the leader who struggled with Gladstone for Irish Home Rule and who died in 1907 before seeing to what depths that struggle for independence had come:

> What need you, being come to sense,
> But fumble in a greasy till
> And add the halfpence to the pence
> And prayer to shivering prayer until
> You have dried the marrow from the bone;
> For men were born to pray and save:
> Romantic Ireland's dead and gone;
> It's with O'Leary in the grave.

Even before the beginning of the 1916 fighting, three events seemed to Yeats emblematic of a coarsened spirit in Ireland. The first was the desecration of Parnell, one of the foremost nationalist leaders, who, at the height of his popularity and political power, had been discovered to be having an affair with a married woman. As soon as this scandal was revealed, Parnell was pulled down by the mob and driven into exile. Yeats was appalled at the hypocrisy and fickleness of press and people, abandoning a man whom a moment before they had seemed to idolize.

The second event was the rejection of Sir Hugh Lane's bequest of his magnificent collection of pictures: the gift was turned down by the Dublin Corporation on the grounds that the city rates would have to be raised in order to buy a site and build an art gallery. This convinced Yeats of the new philistinism of Ireland ('fumble in a greasy till'). The third event (and the one closest to Yeats's heart) was the violent reception given to Synge's play *The Playboy of the Western World*. Synge had long been a friend of Yeats; they had shared lodgings when Synge was in his early twenties. Yeats had encouraged Synge in his writing, especially in his interest in Irish dialect and folk-lore. *The Playboy of the Western World* drew on the peasantry of the west of Ireland, whose speech and traditions meant so much to Yeats—their racy talk, their stories, their delight in audacity for its own sake, even their emotional gullibility; Yeats had tried to reflect some of this in his own verse drama, but acknowledged that he had been less successful than Synge. Yet when Synge's play was performed, it was taken by the Irish nationalist press to be a slur on Ireland, with Irishmen being presented as rustic fools, ignorant simpletons, stage comics. The play was booed off the stage, in the Dublin theatre, the Abbey, which Yeats had promoted with dedication. Everywhere the mob seemed to have triumphed. Yeats saw in 'the leaders of the crowd' who had achieved this that

> They must to keep their certainty accuse
> All that are different of a base intent;
> Pull down established honour; hawk for news
> Whatever their loose fantasy invent
> And murmur it with bated breath . . .

But Yeats's link with Irish nationalism was not just one of disillusioned patriotic sentiment; it was also one of love. He had fallen in love with Maud Gonne at their first meeting in 1889. For years they were associated together in Yeats's work for the theatre, in nationalist political and literary meetings all over Ireland. Yet his love was a hopeless one; she always refused to marry him and, quite suddenly in 1903, married instead one of the Irish nationalist leaders, John MacBride. The woman he had exalted to the position of his Muse became a rabble-rouser. But he did not blame her (despite the lines I have quoted about her from 'A Prayer for my Daughter'), nor in this case did he blame Ireland; he blamed himself, his timidity, his naivety, his ignorance of the world and of 'reality'.

What he learned to do in his poetry was to face himself, his complexities and inconsistencies, in a harsh and even pitiless confrontation. This is the theme of one of his last poems, 'The Circus Animals' Desertion'—the abandonment of 'allegorical dreams' and the realization that

> I must lie down where all the ladders start,
> In the foul rag-and-bone shop of the heart.

Alongside this self-confrontation goes an almost tragic sense of history as a series of patterns of behaviour and action. Man's life is controlled by forces of destiny outside himself; the gyres or circles of history are continually turning, dragging in their wake a succession of consequences; what has happened will happen again.

This pattern of destiny or succession of consequences is the theme of his strange, powerful sonnet 'Leda and the Swan' and of 'The Second Coming'. Leda, a beautiful Queen of Sparta, was (according to legend) noticed by Zeus, the greatest of the gods on Olympus, who descended to earth in the form of a swan and raped her. Leda consequently gave birth to two eggs, from one of which Helen was born—Helen, whose seduction by Paris was the cause of the Trojan War, which in its turn caused the birth of the Greek nation, which in its turn laid the foundations of modern Europe ... and so on. The poem first gives a violent sensual picture of the rape itself, the clash between animal and human, God and man. Implicit in the picture (and it *is* pictorial, as if one of the classic representations of 'Leda and the Swan' in a painting is being evoked) and in the act itself is the realization that from it will result Love and War, the two activities which Helen symbolizes; so that the birth of western civilization is also the birth of two of man's primary passions, lust and violence. Zeus, as the supreme god, must have realized these consequences, but did Leda, the passive woman through whom history enacted itself?

> Did she put on his knowledge with his power
> Before the indifferent beak could let her drop?

This clash of human and divine also suggests a greater Annunciation—that of Mary the mother of Christ; but in 'The Second Coming' this has been brutalized and turned awry—'Mere anarchy is loosed upon the world'—and in its wake comes a more terrible revelation:

>   but now I know
> That twenty centuries of stony sleep
> Were vexed to nightmare by a rocking cradle,
> And what rough beast, its hour come round at last,
> Slouches towards Bethlehem to be born?

Much of Yeats's later poetry—and some of it is likely to be among his most enduring—stems not from political or historical or mystical thought, or from his frustrated love for Maud Gonne, but from the unquenchable and unsatisfied *generalized* passion of his old age:

> You think it horrible that lust and rage
> Should dance attention upon my old age;
> They were not such a plague when I was young;
> What else have I to spur me into song?

The poems in *Words for Music Perhaps, A Woman Young and Old,* and *Last Poems* can be seen as the crowning success in Yeats's search for a *persona,* or mask: the projection of a situation and a voice into other people—Crazy Jane, the Lady and the Chambermaid. He dramatized his own desires, and set them in the body and spirit and words of a woman, as in 'The Lady's First Song':

> I turn round
> Like a dumb beast in a show,
> Neither know what I am
> Nor where I go,
> My language beaten
> Into one name;
> I am in love
> And that is my shame.
> What hurts the soul
> My soul adores,
> No better than a beast
> Upon all fours.

At their most extreme, these late poems seem to reject any view of man (and woman) other than as a simple, desiring animal. The 'responsibilities' of politics which earlier had so exercised him were reduced to the primary passions. Taking some words by Thomas Mann as his epigraph—'In our time the destiny of man presents itself in political terms'—he wrote his poem 'Politics'. The scene is a party, full of distinguished, knowledge-able (and opinionated) men—politicians, men of affairs, journalists—discussing the world situation: this was the 1930s, with the Second World War on the horizon. Yeats sees near him a young and beautiful girl, and her presence distracts him from the abstract talk, so that he cannot fix his attention

> On Roman or on Russian
> Or on Spanish politics.
> Yet here's a travelled man that knows
> What he talks about,
> And there's a politician
> That has read and thought,
> And maybe what they say is true
> Of war and war's alarms
> But O that I were young again
> And held her in my arms!

This too can be seen as, if not exactly a pose, then not the whole story either; in a letter written at almost the same time, he said:

> Do not try to make a politician of me, even in Ireland I shall never I think be that again—as my sense of reality deepens, and I think it does with age, my horror at the cruelty of governments grows greater . . . I am not callous, every nerve trembles with horror at what is happening in Europe, 'the ceremony of innocence is drowned'.

His sense of reality had indeed deepened; his prophetic side (embodied in that quotation from his own 'The Second Coming' in the letter) had taken a much firmer and more deliberate grip on the real. For over fifty years he had struggled in his art 'to condense as out of the flying vapour of the world an image of human perfection'—an ambition as much of the Renaissance as of the Romantic age. 'Themes . . . that might adorn old songs or courtly shows' were not rejected but transmuted in 'the fury and the mire of human veins'. He took the colloquial and raised it to rhetoric; he hammered the disparate images of his life into a unity which was more than the sum of its parts. Soon after Yeats's death in January 1939, T. S. Eliot wrote:

> There are some poets whose poetry can be considered in isolation, for experience and delight. There are others whose poetry, though

giving equally experience and delight, has a larger historical importance. Yeats was one of the latter: he was one of the few whose history is the history of their own time, who are part of the consciousness of an age which cannot be understood without them. This is a very high position to assign to him: but I believe that it is one which is secure.

CHAPTER FOUR

Wilfred Owen (1893–1918)
Edward Thomas (1878–1917)
D. H. Lawrence (1885–1930)

Most of the poems we now think of as being both typical of the
First World War and its best literary representations were not
written until after the Battle of the Somme in 1916. Until then
most English poets, good and bad, old and young, civilian or
military, had—if they wrote about the war at all—written about
it with patriotic fervour. Even Hardy, in his 'Men Who March
Away', showed an untypical spirit of religious rectitude:

> In our heart of hearts believing
> Victory crowns the just,
> And that braggarts must
> Surely bite the dust.

The young poet who most quickly seemed to catch the mood of
the moment was Rupert Brooke. Even before his death in 1915,
he had became almost a legend: strikingly handsome, intelligent,
enthusiastic, his poetry seemed to many people at that time to
have an Elizabethan vigour. Two of his sonnets from the short
sequence called *1914* are still known by millions whom poetry
does not otherwise touch: 'Peace' and 'The Soldier':

> If I should die, think only this of me:
> That there's some corner of a foreign field
> That is for ever England.

Julian Grenfell, who was killed in Flanders in 1915, had the same
feeling of war as a noble adventure, even—at a lower level—as
boyish fun: 'I *adore* war. It is like a big picnic without the object-
lessness of a picnic.' In his poem 'Into Battle', he wrote:

> And life is colour and warmth and light,
> And a striving evermore for these;
> And he is dead who will not fight;
> And who dies fighting has increase.

But by 1916 it had become almost impossible for either soldiers or civilians to think of war as 'a big picnic' or a gallant crusade, with the young English combatants 'as swimmers into cleanness leaping'. The trench warfare and the battles dragged on, the casualty lists grew bigger and bigger, and poets such as Siegfried Sassoon and Edmund Blunden (and, a little earlier, Charles Sorley) began to express in their poetry more realistically and satirically the waste and horror of war. It is Wilfred Owen, however, who has come to be seen as the finest poet of the war period, though it took some time after his death in November 1918 and the publication of his *Poems* in 1920 for his importance to be widely recognized.

Up until about 1916, Owen was a fairly conventional poet, immersed in Keats and Tennyson and imitating them. He had spent a short time in France just before the war, teaching and studying, and it is there that he began to use his characteristic half-rhymes, possibly in imitation of certain French poems to which he had been introduced by a literary French friend. The device at first was used quite deliberately, in the nature of an ingenious technical exercise:

> Leaves
>   Murmuring by myriads in the shimmering trees.
> Lives
>   Wakening with wonder in the Pyrenees.
> Birds
>   Cheerily chirping in the early day.
> Bards
>   Singing of summer scything thro' the hay . . .

But the trick came to be more than simply a trick: Edmund Blunden, who edited the first attempt at a complete edition of Owen's poems, commented that 'again and again by means of it he creates remoteness, darkness, emptiness, shock, echo, the last word'. Faced with the appalling life of an infantryman in France, he toughened and matured. A little over a year before his death, he wrote in a letter:

> Tennyson, it seems, was always a great child. So should I have been, but for Beaumont Hamel [a part of the front line in France where there was particularly heavy fighting]. Not before January 1917 did I write the *only* lines of mine that carry the stamp of maturity.

The lines he refers to are from 'Happiness', written shortly before 'Exposure', one of his best poems. In the brief period of less than two years during which he wrote all the poems by which he is best known, he grew, not in sensitiveness—that was there already, in the Keats-and-Tennyson poems—but in depth; his innate romantic and sensuous temperament was disciplined and made more powerful by coming to terms with a reality that was always harsh and often tragic:

> Our brains ache, in the merciless iced east winds that knive us . . .
> Wearied we keep awake because the night is silent . . .
> Low, drooping flares confuse our memory of the salient . . .
> Worried by silence, sentries whisper, curious, nervous,
> But nothing happens.

Yet the romanticism was still there; and it was this which Yeats was really criticizing when he refused to include any of Owen's poems in the *Oxford Book of Modern Verse* as late as 1936. He refers elsewhere (in one of his letters to Dorothy Wellesley) to Owen's poetry as 'all blood, dirt and sucked sugar stick . . . he calls poets "bards", a girl a "maid" and talks about "Titanic wars". There is every excuse for him but none for those who like him.' Yeats's notion of the hero, and his increased effort in his own diction to use the sinewy colloquial, could not comprehend or sympathize with a romanticism so different from his own. To Yeats, Owen's compassion seemed mere self-pity and morbid self-indulgence, his language the remnants of outworn nineteenth-century fashions. But Owen had his own answer, ignored by Yeats, in the preface written when he was gathering his poems together for a possible book:

> This book is not about heroes. English Poetry is not yet fit to
> speak of them.
> Nor is it about legends, or lands, or anything about glory,
> honour, might, majesty, dominion, or power, except War.
> Above all, I am not concerned with Poetry.
> My subject is War, and the pity of War.
> The Poetry is in the pity.
> Yet these elegies are to this generation in no sense consolatory.
> They may be to the next. All a poet can do to-day is warn.
> That is why the true Poets must be truthful.

'Above all, I am not concerned with Poetry'; by this he means
attitudinizing about war, romance putting the gilt on reality:

> But they are troops who fade, not flowers
> For poets' tearful fooling.

The poet's job is not to embroider but to warn; and the monitory,
didactic, moralizing element is strong in Owen's poems. They
are true to their period, too, and in few cases could they have
been written under the very different circumstances of the Second
World War; they are products of the wastefulness, dirt, muddle
and boredom of trench warfare. What action there is tends to be
brutish and unheroic, as in 'Mental Cases', 'S.I.W.', 'The Dead
Beat', 'À Terre', and, more impersonal and less fiercely and
savagely indignant, 'Strange Meeting', an encounter as if in a
dream between an English soldier and the German soldier whom
he has killed:

> 'I am the enemy you killed, my friend.
> I knew you in this dark: for so you frowned
> Yesterday through me as you jabbed and killed.
> I parried; but my hands were loath and cold.
> Let us sleep now . . .'

There are others, such as 'Inspection', which are quite as colloquial, satirical and sharp as anything Sassoon ever wrote.
Indeed, the personal and literary influence of Sassoon on Owen
was strong. They saw a good deal of one another during one
stage of the war, when they were in the same officers' hospital.
Something of what Owen felt for Sassoon (who was older and

who already had some reputation as a poet), and something of the individuality of Owen's letters, can be seen in the following excerpt from a letter to his fellow-patient, written after he had left hospital:

> Know that since mid-September, when you still regarded me as a tiresome little knocker on your door, I held you as Keats + Christ + Elijah + my colonel + my father-confessor + Amenophis IV in profile. What's that mathematically?

But Owen went beyond Sassoon. As Philip Larkin has put it:

> While Sassoon sought to turn the insensitivity that permitted the continuance of the war into disgust, Owen tried to turn it into compassion. Sassoon concentrated on the particular ('When Dick was killed last week he looked like that, / Flapping along the firestep like a fish'); Owen deliberately discarded all but generalities.

What Larkin calls the 'extraordinary resonance' that this withdrawal into impersonality gives can be seen in 'Insensibility'. The loose line structure and the variable stresses echo the mingled doubt and definitiveness of what is being said:

> Happy are men who yet before they are killed
> Can let their veins run cold.
> Whom no compassion fleers
> Or makes their feet
> Sore on the alleys cobbled with their brothers.
> The front line withers,
> But they are troops who fade, not flowers
> For poets' tearful fooling:
> Men, gaps for filling:
> Losses who might have fought
> Longer; but no one bothers.

And later:

> Having seen all things red,
> Their eyes are rid
> Of the hurt of the colour of blood for ever.

Here the two short lines with their monosyllabic half-rhymes stab home quickly before the long line, whose disillusionment and weariness is stressed by that very length and by the repeated

'of ... of ... of', throwing the stress on to 'hurt ... colour ...
blood' and dying away in the hardly stressed 'for ever'. And in
the final stanza Owen moves with absolute sureness to a
heightened conclusion which takes large romantic abstractions
that have completely detached themselves from his infatuation
with Keats and Tennyson:

> By choice they made themselves immune
> To pity and whatever mourns in man
> Before the last sea and the hapless stars;
> Whatever mourns when many leave these shores;
> Whatever shares
> The eternal reciprocity of tears.

It is almost inevitable that one should bring Keats into any
discussion of Owen, not only because of the early influence but
because the rapid transformation from a stage of pleasant but
immature sensuous literariness to that of becoming a major poet
seems so similar in both. In their mid-twenties they suddenly
flowered, and died. What Owen would have done, how he
would have written, what he would have written about, if he
had survived into the post-war world, are of course impossible
speculations. To the poets of the 1930s (in particular Auden and
Day Lewis) Owen was an inspiration. His work survives and
lives today not just as a 'war poet', nor even as *the* 'war poet',
though a particular war was the subject-matter of his best poems.
To quote Larkin again:

> ... in the end Owen's war is not Sassoon's war but all war; not
> particular suffering but all suffering; not particular waste but all
> waste.

EDWARD THOMAS

Another poet who was killed during the First World War was
Edward Thomas. Thomas began to write poetry late, and for most
of his life he earned a precarious living with all kinds of literary

and topographical journalism. The American poet Robert Frost, who was living in England between 1912 and 1915, encouraged him, for they shared a sympathy of mood and subject: the slow deliberate ways of the country and its seasons and traditions were common to both poets. Yet it is not as a simple rural poet that Thomas, any more than Frost, should be valued. What is impressive in such a piece as 'Old Man' is the tentative, digressive way in which Thomas winds himself into the poem, the movement following hesitant speech rhythms, and the sharp concreteness of observation which yet allows room for mystery. It proceeds rationally but is aware of the irrational. The herb is seen, touched, smelt with delicate precision; and the imagined child and the watching poet are blended and then dramatically set apart at the line break

> As for myself
> Where first I met the bitter herb is lost.

The hesitation opens out from there to a cumulative sense of loss, emptiness, disturbance, even horror:

> No garden appears, no path, no hoar-green bush
> Of Lad's-love, or Old Man, no child beside,
> Neither father nor mother, nor any playmate;
> Only an avenue, dark, nameless, without end.

Edward Thomas's best poems have the air of being what F. R. Leavis has called 'a random jotting down of chance impressions and sensations, the record of a moment of relaxed and undirected consciousness'. Sometimes they stay, simply and perfectly, at the level of perception, of noticing some minute adjustment or juxtaposition which reveals a sensuous truth, as in 'Tall Nettles':

> Tall nettles cover up, as they have done
> These many springs, the rusty harrow, the plough
> Long worn out, and the roller made of stone:
> Only the elm butt tops the nettles now.
>
> This corner of the farmyard I like most:
> As well as any bloom upon a flower
> I like the dust on the nettles, never lost
> Except to prove the sweetness of a shower.

Other poems, such as 'I Never Saw That Land Before' and 'The Owl', have a more direct human poignancy, with the observed scene and its reflections mingled. The owl is an unmoralizing reminder, with its cry out in the night, of the deprivation that lies beyond comfort, just as 'that land' is caught in acute physical description simply because it was transient, caught at first sight and now only in the mind.

There are two other broad groups of poems: the love poems and the longer blank-verse narratives. I find the love poems on the whole Thomas's least successful work, though they have been much praised. For me there is something too thin, too fey and sentimental, about them; they share characteristics with the Georgian poets with whom Thomas used to be grouped (though he was never included in any of Marsh's anthologies of *Georgian Poetry*) before the re-awakening of interest in his work during the 1950s. But the narrative blank-verse poems, such as 'As the Team's Head-Brass' and 'Wind and Mist', are masterly in their control, and here again one must speak of Frost, for it was Frost supremely who could handle this sort of thing and Thomas must have learned much from him. It is perhaps wrong to put the emphasis on 'narrative'; rather, they are anecdotes, accounts of incidents which share with the shorter poems a feeling of sensations observed and things noticed. The conversation between the poet and the ploughman in 'As the Team's Head-Brass'—

> One minute and an interval of ten,
> A minute more and the same interval—

follows the leisurely progress of the plough, against which is set the sporadic and laconic talk of the war: what is happening here is timeless, regular as the seasons, and that very fact underlines the melancholy of the scene:

> The horses started and for the last time
> I watched the clods crumble and topple over
> After the ploughshare and the stumbling team.

One of Thomas's best pieces lies in none of these areas: the long poem 'Lob', written in easy ambling couplets and blending many of Thomas's ideas about mythology, folklore, landscape and the continuity of all these. Lob seems to be a real man, or an amalgam of real men, but he is also part of history and even what went before history. He is everywhere and everything in rural England:

> Before all other men
> 'Twas he first called the Hog's Back the Hog's Back.
> That Mother Dunch's Buttocks should not lack
> Their name was his care. He too could explain
> Totteridge and Totterdown and Juggler's Lane:
> He knows, if anyone. Why Tumbling Bay,
> Inland in Kent, is called so, he might say.

Thomas's special achievement in his poems was the rare one of speaking with an unforced, unrhetorical voice which is at the same time memorable in its timbre and cadences. Rhythmically, he is one of the subtlest poets in English; his language (with the exception of a handful of rather awkward archaisms and whimsies) is precise, evocative and haunting. His most characteristic subject-matter—the whole sense of rural England—was endangered when he wrote and is rapidly being engulfed now; only such a poet as his namesake, R. S. Thomas in rural Wales, can nowadays come unselfconsciously close to such concerns. Edward Thomas's poems have little to do with 'the modern movement', with Eliot and Pound who were writing at the time, yet they are quite centrally part of an English tradition that continues today. As early as 1927, when they were undergraduates at Oxford, Auden and Day Lewis included Thomas in the 'extremely short' list of 'contemporary poets whom we had little or no hope of ever equalling'. It has been maintained by Edna Longley that 'both Philip Larkin and Ted Hughes, two of the best contemporary English poets, might easily trace an ancestry back to different aspects of Edward Thomas': one might think of Larkin's 'Here' and 'An Arundel Tomb', and of Hughes's 'The Bull Moses', as exemplifying this. The materials are different but the manner is pervasive.

D. H. LAWRENCE

D. H. Lawrence was not, of course, primarily a poet; his main reputation rests on his novels and stories, and to some extent on his essays and plays. Yet he began as a poet, wrote poems throughout his life, and the temper and atmosphere of his prose fiction is very often poetic. Edmund Wilson, the American critic, has written:

> Would not D. H. Lawrence . . . if he had lived a century earlier, probably have told his tales, as Byron and Crabbe did, in verse? Is it not just as correct to consider him the last of the great English romantic poets as one of the most original of modern English novelists?

But, if one makes any formal distinction between the techniques of poetry and prose, Lawrence was seldom a great poet. His sensibility, his intensity, his impressionistic and symbolical gifts (to take just one example, the scene in *Women in Love* where Birkin throws stones into the moon's reflection in a pool), his sometimes dithyrambic rhythms and his verbal repetitions—all these, in his fiction, are *close* to poetry, or are part of the raw material of poetry; but Lawrence, when writing poetry as such, seldom paid enough attention to received forms to shape his ideas into more than notes towards poems. Indeed, he despised what I call received forms: 'Remember, skilled verse is dead in fifty years.' What he aimed at, he said, was 'a free, essential verse, that cuts to the centre of things'. It was through Walt Whitman's example (as Lawrence himself acknowledged) that he came to find the kind of patterning that could be 'direct utterance from the instant, whole man'.

Lawrence's best poems are those which keep their eyes firmly on the object, describing and evoking without too much of a didactic or moralizing burden. Several of the pieces in *Birds, Beasts and Flowers* come into this category: 'Snake', 'Kangaroo', 'The Mosquito', 'Bat'. The moralizing element is there in all of them, but there is also enough natural perception (the way a snake drinks, the way a kangaroo hops, the way a mosquito approaches its victim, the way a bat swoops) to make a firm basis, a logical jumping-off place, for the moral. In 'Snake', for example:

> He lifted his head from drinking, as cattle do,
> And looked at me vaguely, as drinking cattle do,
> And flickered his two-forked tongue from his lips, and mused a
> > moment,
> And stooped and drank a little more,
> Being earth-brown, earth-golden from the burning bowels of the
> > earth
> On the day of Sicilian July, with Etna smoking.

That is accurately and beautifully said, the lines marvellously miming the action and the observation; the 'evidence' is there to experience the conclusion—that, after frightening away the snake,

> > . . . immediately I regretted it.
> I thought how paltry, how vulgar, what a mean act!
> I despised myself and the voices of my accursed human education . . .
> And so, I missed my chance with one of the lords
> Of life.
> And I have something to expiate;
> A pettiness.

'Bavarian Gentians' and, at greater length and more ambitiously, 'The Ship of Death', are free verse poems that less visually but with almost equal power move with a controlled sinuous rhetoric. There are other poems, most of them among his early work, which are concerned with making a more formal statement, and yet which keep a vividness and freshness that come from personal observation. Such poems are 'Piano' and 'Discord in Childhood'; 'The Collier's Wife', a narrative in his native Nottinghamshire dialect; and 'Giorno Dei Morti', written during his first stay in Italy in 1912–13 and describing an Italian country funeral:

> > Along the avenue of cypresses,
> > All in their scarlet cloaks and surplices
> > Of linen, go the chanting choristers,
> > The priests in gold and black, the villagers . . .

> And all along the path to the cemetery
> The round dark heads of men crowd silently
> And black-scarved faces of women, wistfully
> Watch at the banner of death, and the mystery.
>
> And at the foot of a grave a father stands
> With sunken head, and forgotten, folded hands;
> And at the foot of a grave a mother kneels
> With pale shut face, nor either hears nor feels
>
> The coming of the chanting choristers
> Between the avenue of cypresses,
> The silence of the many villagers,
> The candle-flames beside the surplices.

This seems to bear out what Geoffrey Grigson has said of Lawrence's poems: 'the stronger the emotion, the more defined the structure'. Such firm definition can be found in poems that are more obviously close to Lawrence's primary emotions than the beautiful but distanced 'Giorno Dei Morti': for example in 'Last Words to Miriam' (the Miriam of *Sons and Lovers*), and in 'The Bride' and 'Hymn to Priapus', which concern his mother.

In the totally 'free' poems, there is often too much unsupported statement, too much badgering of the reader and hammering of the insistent point; the tone of voice becomes harsh, strained and, in the end, nagging:

> I wish people, when you sit near them,
> wouldn't think it necessary to make conversation
> and send thin draughts of words
> blowing down your neck and your ears
> and giving you a cold in your inside.

It is as if the looseness and staccato quality of much of his free verse came not from pressure of feeling—the words forcing themselves down, impatient of constraint—but from sheer exasperated *lack* of real motive or impulse; so that they are petulant notes on, rather than transmutations of, sensations and moods. This is particularly true of the poems in *Pansies* (a cheeky twisting of *pensées*), which are mostly not only petulant but petty.

In the foreword he wrote to *Pansies* (which appeared in 1929, the year before his death), Lawrence made clear his own attitude towards what he was up to—something provisional, not permanent:

> Anyhow, I offer a bunch of pansies, not a wreath of *immortelles*. I don't want everlasting flowers, and I don't want to offer them to anybody else. A flower passes, and that perhaps is the best of it. If we can take it in its transience, its breath, its maybe mephistophelian, maybe palely ophelian face, the look it gives, the gestures of its full bloom, and the way it turns upon us to depart—that was the flower, we have had it, and no *immortelle* can give us anything in comparison. The same with the pansy poems; merely the breath of the moment, and one eternal moment easily contradicting the next eternal moment. Only don't nail the pansy down. You won't keep it any better if you do.

This is said with typical brusque assurance, almost charmingly; but in the event it isn't quite convincing. The Lawrence poems that truly survive—the best of *Birds, Beasts and Flowers*, some early ones (among which one ought to include 'The Best of School' and 'Last Lesson of the Afternoon'), and a handful of strongly patterned later ones—do so because they *do* catch and fix an 'eternal moment'. And taken together they form, even more than the novels and stories, what Lawrence called 'a biography of an emotional and inner life'.

CHAPTER FIVE

T. S. Eliot (1888–1965)

In a broadcast tribute made just after T. S. Eliot's death early in 1965, W. H. Auden countered Eliot's own one-time labelling of himself as 'a classicist':

> This seems to me misleading because, whatever he may have intended by the term, it inevitably suggests a poet whose work can be viewed as a logical and inevitable step in the historical development of English poetry. To me, on the contrary, he seems one of the most idiosyncratic of poets, both in his subject matter and in his technique.

Auden went on to say that he had the impression that, like Wordsworth, Eliot's 'inspiration for nearly all he wrote arose out of a few intense visionary experiences, which probably occurred quite early in life'.

This remark by Auden, linking Eliot's idiosyncrasy with a few early and intense 'spots of time' such as Wordsworth celebrated in *The Prelude*, is for me an illuminating one. But thought about in the light of Eliot's criticism—criticism which has been as influential as his poetry—it is unlikely that Eliot himself would quite have agreed. A great deal of that criticism is concerned to show that 'the progress of an artist is a continual self-sacrifice, a continual extinction of personality'; it states as an axiom that 'the more perfect the artist, the more completely separate in him will be the man who suffers and the mind which creates; the more perfectly will the mind digest and transmute the passions which are its material'.

In Eliot's lifetime (and the effect is still there, even at this distance from his death), readers were perhaps so convinced by these magisterial pronouncements that they were scared off trying to make any relationship between Eliot's life and his poetry. But as Philip Larkin has put it, 'Separating the man who suffers from the mind which creates is all right—we separate the petrol from the engine—but the dependence of the second on the first is complete.' Until there is an authoritative biography of Eliot (and perhaps not even then), we can work only by intelligent hints, and by thinking about the growth of his mind and his sensibility in the development of what we *do* know about his life. An American who became British, and in the process became specifically a devout member of the Church of England; a man of serious scholarly discipline who also relished childishness and even ribaldry; a conservative whose effect on his time was revolutionary; a private man who spent most of his life in public positions, as editor and publisher; a husband haunted and tortured by the experience and memory of his first marriage until, late in life, he found fulfilment in his second—all these aspects of Eliot the man are revealed in Eliot the poet and critic.

But 'revealed' is too dramatic a word, and also too glib. Eliot was at pains not only to transmute raw life into distanced art, but to emphasize how inevitable the difficulty of the end-product was. In his essay on the Metaphysical poets (1921), he wrote:

> We can only say that it appears likely that poets in our civilization, as it exists at present, must be *difficult*. Our civilization comprehends great variety and complexity, and that variety and complexity, playing upon a refined sensibility, must produce various and complex results. The poet must become more and more comprehensive, more allusive, more indirect, in order to force, to dislocate if necessary, language into his meaning.

In fact a sense of struggle, a sense of complex tactics employed in attempting to tame a recalcitrant animal, is one of the marks of Eliot's poetry, as early as the sardonic self-questioning of Prufrock in 'The Love Song of J. Alfred Prufrock' (written in 1910–11) and as late as the last of the *Four Quartets*, 'Little Gidding', written over thirty years later. There is, of course, a considerable difference between the tremulous 'Shall I . . .?' and 'Would it . . .?' expressions of Prufrock and the 'We shall not cease from exploration . . .' passage in 'Little Gidding'; but in both the emphasis is on laboriousness and circuitousness.

Though in many ways he became rooted in England and in

English institutions, there was nothing parochially English about Eliot's attitudes. Born in the Middle West of the United States, but of New England stock and educated in New England for most of his school and early university years, he was from the beginning caught between two backgrounds. In 1930, three years after he had become a British citizen, he wrote:

> Of course, my people were northerners and New Englanders, and of course I have spent many years out of America altogether; but Missouri and the Mississippi have made a deeper impression on me than any other part of the world.

Long after his first experience of these two widely separated landscapes of America, the two flow together in the water imagery of 'The Dry Salvages': in it, the sea references are all obviously to the New England coast (Eliot's own preliminary note about the title makes this clear), and the river references just as obviously draw on the Mississippi–Missouri.

From Harvard, at which he studied philosophy, he went on to further studies in Paris, Munich, Marburg and Oxford. By this time, 1914, the First World War had begun. In England he married, began to earn a living (first as a schoolmaster, then as a bank employee), and also began to publish—a handful of poems on which he had been working between 1909 and 1911, but which were not seen in print, in various magazines, until 1915: 'Preludes', 'Portrait of a Lady', 'The Love Song of J. Alfred Prufrock' and 'Rhapsody on a Windy Night'. Ezra Pound, also an American cultural *emigré*, was an early champion of these first poems: an indefatigable discoverer, promoter and literary stage-manager, he was quick to see Eliot's originality and to make sure that others did too.

As early as these poems published in 1915, a characteristic Eliot method is apparent: the impressionistic juxtaposition of references to other works, sometimes direct, sometimes oblique. In 'Prufrock', for example, there is first of all the epigraph from Dante—continuingly one of Eliot's great masters and exemplars; and then, in the body of the poem, quotations from or echoes of the Bible, Shakespeare, Donne and others. It is a method we associate much more with music than with literature (the 'quotation' of a theme by one composer in the work of another), and, though Eliot always disclaimed a deep technical knowledge of music, the musical analogies—in structure, in rhythm, even in inspiration—are there in his poems. (And see his 1942 essay, 'The Music of Poetry'.)

Among the 1915 poems, 'Prufrock' and 'Portrait of a Lady' are what one might call half-dramatized monologues, while 'Preludes' and 'Rhapsody on a Windy Night' are fragmentary lyrics, evocations of terror or unease in banal urban settings. All are poems for a single voice. A few years later when he wrote 'The Waste Land', he moved into an area which continued to fascinate him for the rest of his writing life—that of drama. Not that 'The Waste Land' is in any sense a play as the five works from *Murder in the Cathedral* to *The Elder Statesman* are plays. But it *is* many-voiced in its attack, like a fragmentary play of which the list of *dramatis personae* has been lost. To read the full transcript version of the poem as it was first published in 1971, set side-by-side with the work as it was known from its publication in 1922, is fascinating: it shows how (chiefly through Pound's brisk but sensitive guidance) a rather shapeless and sprawling sequence was pared down to the difficult but unified poem we know.

'The Waste Land' is often regarded as being primarily a reflection of twentieth-century disillusionment and despair, and of course it does include these elements; hence its success as a 'universal' poem, translated into many languages and influential in the work of many poets. But late in his life Eliot remarked on it in this way:

> Various critics have done me the honour to interpret the poem in terms of criticism of the contemporary world, have considered it, indeed, as an important bit of social criticism. To me it was only the relief of a personal and wholly insignificant grouse against life; it is just a piece of rhythmical grumbling.

Such pawky modesty is partly intended to disconcert, of course: the poem was fair game for researchers and commentators of all kinds, and Eliot was from time to time part defensive, part facetious, in his written and recorded comments on it. See, for example, his humorously dismissive reference to the notes he attached to 'The Waste Land', in his 1956 lecture on 'The Frontiers of Criticism'. These were, I think, the tactics of a man who was not only weary of solemn or over-ingenious interpretation but embarrassed by the objective weight which had been given to a poem which had had its release, if not its origin, in an acute state of nervous mental stress and depression, aggravated by his first wife's own psychological state. This is not an explanation of 'The Waste Land'; it does not pretend to spell out glibly what the poem is 'about'. But perhaps it does help to explain Eliot's gently exasperated impatience with the kind of exegesis which sees it in terms of quasi-scriptural text for the twentieth century.

Despite Eliot's derogatory remarks about them, the notes do contain some significant pointers. The two books to which he refers at the beginning of the notes (Jessie Weston's *From Ritual to Romance* and Sir James Frazer's *The Golden Bough*) are anthropological studies of myth. The parts of these books on which 'The Waste Land' draws are concerned with vegetation myths, in which the cycle of the seasons, of natural growth, death and renewal, are seen in terms of human manifestation—in sex, in kingship and law, and in religion. In 'The Waste Land', the ritual order linking nature and man in a divine bond has been broken; there is sterility, anarchy and a sense of loss. This loss is ironically put in terms of the primitive and prehistoric myths themselves, thrown into contrast with conflicting images from past literature, from fragments of songs and scriptures (both Christian and non-Christian), from history and from modern life.

The change of seasons, the beginning of new growth, are seen from the start as something painful:

> April is the cruellest month, breeding
> Lilacs out of the dead land, mixing
> Memory and desire, stirring
> Dull roots with spring rain . . .

Memory and desire are two of several forces in opposition in 'The Waste Land'. Pangs of nostalgia (the hyacinth girl in 'The Burial of the Dead', 'the pleasant whining of a mandoline' in 'The Fire Sermon', the boat in 'What the Thunder said') jostle with memories of horror and emptiness (the encounter with Stetson in 'The Burial of the Dead', 'I remember/Those are pearls that were his eyes' in 'A Game of Chess', the songs of the three Thames Daughters in 'The Fire Sermon'). But the memories are fragmentary, jarring, meaningless; they form nothing coherent; they are 'broken images'.

It is difficult, perhaps impossible, with 'The Waste Land' to find some middle ground between providing a patient but in the end bewildering line-by-line 'information guide' on the one hand and an extensive moralizing commentary on the other. The first is at least preferable to the second, because it can leave interpretation to the reader; though the danger here is that the 'facts' (a line from Verlaine refers to Wagner's *Parsifal*, which in turn leads us to the Grail Legend and the Fisher King, and so forth) too thoroughly clog the reading eye, making the poem static when it is kaleidoscopic and dynamic. As for commentary, it can sometimes march side by side with the poem, but it can never be a substitute for it; paraphrase usually serves to show only that Eliot wrote what he did and as he did because it was most economical and most arresting. (Here again, Pound's function was to concentrate and sharpen.)

It may be useful, though, to consider briefly the particular *manner* of one part, Part 2, 'A Game of Chess'. In Part 1, 'The Burial of the Dead', it is chiefly the land that is seen as barren. Now, attention is focused on the sterility of *human* life. The section begins with an opulent description of the room of a rich woman, recalling Cleopatra and Dido; both have a reputation for being great lovers, great courtesans, out of an historical and almost mythical past. But the modern woman who inhabits this room exists in the middle of sterile splendour; for example, the Cupidon (love-god) is golden—an expensive ornament, with no living significance to the woman. The descriptive lines (77–96) are like something from a Ben Jonson play (compare the description of wealth in *Volpone*) but, as in Jonson, the lavishness of verbal ornamentation serves to emphasize miserliness. In this setting, even the exquisite cries of Philomel, pursued by Tereus, have come to be debased to 'Jug Jug'—not only the conventionalized song of birds in several Elizabethan lyrics but a crude Elizabethan locution for having sex (compare the adoption by the British Army, during the Second World War, of 'Have jig-a-jig, Johnny?'). Philomel is like a nightingale in the desert, a glimpse of forgotten beauty in the waste land.

At this point, the narrative moves from description to an impressionistic treatment of nightmare figures, symbols of the woman's neurosis, and the woman brushes her hair into sparks which

> Glowed into words, then would be savagely still.

The dialogue which follows is a mutually self-enclosed one between the woman and her husband or lover. The woman's words are harsh, abrupt, repetitive: the man's replies are sardonic, perhaps bored, giving nothing away. The eyes of 'the drowned Phoenician Sailor' of 'The Burial of the Dead' (who reappears as the central figure in 'Death by Water') serve only as the background to a jazzy tune in the head, perverting Shakespeare's Ariel dirge from *The Tempest*. The woman's hysteria grows, yet her repeated emphasis on nullity (notice, for example, the repetition of 'nothing' five times in lines 120–123) leads to a plain bald statement of fact—

> The hot water at ten.
> And if it rains, a closed car at four . . .

indications of the emptiness of these lives, with behind them an inexplicable menace—'a knock upon the door'.

The immediate juxtaposition of the working-class scene in the pub heightens the contrast. Here is a world where human beings are sexually fecund, but that very fecundity is wasteful, driving them to an early death. The 'knock upon the door' is not something in the distant future, waiting at the end of almost interminable boredom, but a present reality, implicit in the gruff tones of the publican repeatedly calling out closing-time in the pub: 'HURRY UP PLEASE IT'S TIME.' The scene is implicitly precise, both in time and place, much more closely than any other in the poem; the gossip about Lil and Albert is set in the immediately post-First World War period, and in a London pub; the language is fairly accurately transcribed Cockney (though it is clear from the facsimile transcript of the worksheets that the first Mrs Eliot was a practical help here, ensuring greater accuracy than Eliot himself, still an American and probably bemused by what seemed exoticism, could manage; and Eliot's own recording of the poem, much later, shows an almost comic uncertainty of accent, veering between some sort of Scottish and American Deep South).

Sex is seen vaguely as having 'a good time': what it leads to—attempts at self-induced abortion ('It's them pills I took, to bring it off . . . The chemist said it would be all right, but I've never been the same')—brings in its wake premature ageing. Yet despite the fear, poverty, emptiness, Eliot may perhaps be implying that there is a basic rightness somewhere under these attitudes —'What you get married for if you don't want children?' Rather like the 'Proles' in Orwell's *Nineteen Eighty-Four*, the brutal implication may be that they serve as a fitting contrast to 'the other world'—the world of arid boredom. Their fading farewells merge into the words of Ophelia's farewell in her 'mad scene' (*Hamlet*, Act 4, Scene 5)—words which follow on from her 'and so I thank you for your good counsel'. Lou's and May's advice to Lil is harsh and insensitive; but it is almost as if Eliot is endorsing, with a shudder, that they have the heart of the matter.

These rapid shifts and dislocations, veering from stately iambic pastiche to nervily colloquial staccato exchanges and from obliquely suggested nightmare to greyly recorded documentary, are achieved in less than a hundred lines. There are many other undertones and links with other sections which could be commented on; to take only one example, the connection with the woman in 'What the Thunder said' who 'drew her long black hair out tight' in the parallel nightmare passage of 'voices singing out of empty cisterns and exhausted wells', so that the sterile splendour of the room in 'A Game of Chess' serves to underline the sterility of the 'decayed hole among the mountains' where stands the 'empty chapel', once the home of the Grail (the Chapel Perilous of Arthurian legend). The method of the whole poem is one of interwoven references and reverberations.

Between 'The Waste Land' in the early 1920s and the completion of *Four Quartets* in the early 1940s, Eliot's interest in the drama developed (the choruses for *The Rock* in 1934, and *Murder in the Cathedral* and *The Family Reunion* a few years after that), but some of the most interesting work he wrote was solitary, single-voiced, meditative. In 'The Hollow Men', 'Ash-Wednesday', 'Journey of the Magi' and 'Marina', the soliloquizing of 'Prufrock' and 'Portrait of a Lady' is extended to broader states of mind as he moves towards acceptance of a discipline outside himself. The exhaustion of striving is exchanged for the exhaustion of renunciation ('I no longer strive to strive towards such things': 'Ash Wednesday'). At a distance from these stand the two 'fragments of an Aristophanic melodrama' that make up 'Sweeney Agonistes'—unfinished dramatic pieces showing a development from 'The Waste Land' Eliot might have followed but could not, or at any rate did not. (Some of the cancelled passages in the transcript of 'The Waste Land' read like early attempts to work in this 'Sweeney' area.)

As so often happened with Eliot, ideas and lines rejected from one piece of writing form the nucleus of another; this is what happened with 'Burnt Norton', the first of *Four Quartets*, which Eliot himself said began with fragments discarded from *Murder in the Cathedral*. And, like the different sections of 'The Waste Land', each of the *Four Quartets* can be seen as self-contained yet linked with the others—more precisely in the common patterning into five 'movements' within each poem, each 'movement' having its own recurring structure (the first establishing the poem in its place, the second moving from lyrical meditation to discursive meditation, and so on). This gives a satisfying formal shape to the whole work, yet at the same time allows incidental or subordinate scope, so that we see a mind ranging over personal experiences, over history and the present time, over the struggles of poetry and the difficulties of language, over the sense of place and the sense of time.

In *Four Quartets*, the echoes and allusions are discreet, even sub-dued: conversely, the poet himself is more clearly at the centre of his poem, more palpably transmitting those 'intense visionary experiences' Auden mentioned. Sea, river, garden, tree, bird—each is particularized and illuminated. So 'the word made Flesh' in Part 5 of 'Ash Wednesday', in the midst of doubt and con-fusion, is the central reality in *Four Quartets*—'half guessed . . . half understood', but still a reality. In this, both time and place are given meaning:

> Here the impossible union
> Of spheres of existence is actual,
> Here the past and the future
> Are conquered and reconciled . . .

The triumph is in the reconciliation of opposites—painfully and even brokenly in 'The Waste Land', with grateful humility but without complacency in *Four Quartets*:

> . . . restored by that refining fire
> Where you must move in measure, like a dancer.

To conclude where I began, with Auden's rebuttal of Eliot as a 'classicist', a poet 'whose work can be viewed as a logical and in-evitable step in the historical development of English poetry'. . . . The honours that states and universities heaped on him in the last twenty or so years of his life, the convervatism of his public manner and pronouncements, for many people have obscured the fact that Eliot changed the course of English poetry in a way that no single poet has done since possibly Milton. Eliot was not, and is not, the only genuine model for twentieth-century poetry; but after his example, nothing could be quite the same again. 'The Waste Land', though written so long ago, still strikes one as new and radical, yet at the same time as a classic: every year new generations discover it, are excited by it, and imitate it. Quite apart from abject imitation, one is aware of Eliot as a presence in the most unpredictable places—here and there in Auden, in Dylan Thomas, in John Betjeman, in Philip Larkin, in Ted Hughes.

Unlike the two other revolutionary American poets of his generation, Ezra Pound and William Carlos Williams, he permeated a whole area of the general literary imagination, and goes on doing so: as Helen Gardner (echoing Wordsworth) said of him in the 1940s, 'He has by now created the taste by which he is enjoyed.' Few poets in the history of English literature have managed to do this. Though 'originality' has no particular merit in itself, and most avant-garde writers lack either the talent or the purpose to make the new seem inevitable, Eliot had both immense talent and a firm sense of purpose. He was a revolutionary who survived his own revolution; and though at his death his best work lay some years behind him, right to the end he was aware of his friend Pound's injunction: 'Make it new.'

CHAPTER SIX

W. H. Auden (1907–1973)

A poet's contemporaries (by which I mean not simply those who are alive at the same time but, more narrowly, those who are of the same generation) are not always his best and most accurate judges. They perhaps share too much, have a common topography or stance; or, alternatively, familiarity may breed contempt. In the case of W. H. Auden, his contemporaries accepted and acclaimed him as a master almost from the very beginning. One has only to read the memoirs of Stephen Spender (*World Within World*) and Louis MacNeice (*The Strings are False*), or the early poems of C. Day Lewis, Charles Madge and Rex Warner, to see the impact of Auden while he was still an undergraduate at Oxford. He seemed a severe, omniscient, utterly self-possessed person at the age of nineteen or so, and his success was immediate:

> But there waited for me in the summer morning
> Auden, fiercely. I read, shuddered and knew . . .

Thus Charles Madge, awed into homage by a man who was already a legend in his early twenties. By that time Spender had printed a small book of poems for him on a hand-press, T. S. Eliot had published Auden's charade, *Paid on Both Sides*, in his prestigious magazine *The Criterion*, and in 1930 his first full-scale book, *Poems*, appeared from the publishing house, Faber, of which Eliot was a director.

F. R. Leavis has argued for many years that 'the Auden who conquered the literary world with such ease was the undergraduate intellectual', with all the disabilities of the type—precocious sophistication, lack of real seriousness, 'a surprising radical adolescence that should have been already well outgrown'. What seems particularly to have galled Leavis is what he took to be the smell of conspiracy in the reception that greeted Auden's poetry from the beginning, and that went on greeting it. By 1937—

when Auden was still only thirty—the acclaim was such that the periodical *New Verse* devoted the whole of a special issue to the man, his work, and estimates (mainly congratulatory, though Ezra Pound was indignantly contemptuous) of both. No other English poet of the century has commanded such early and continuous praise. Put in such terms, one can see how Leavis shuddered (with distaste, unlike Charles Madge) at what seemed to be the machinations of a clique, a publicity campaign.

I think Leavis was wrong, and that dislike of a 'system' prevailed over his literary judgement. The Auden that emerged in 1929 and 1930 was indeed more than a prodigy, a university phenomenon, writing work which (in Leavis's opinion) 'might have represented the very green immaturity of a notable creative talent'. Auden's contemporaries did well to be impressed by him, and to take him as their representative voice. The occasional silliness, arrogant obscurity and intellectual pretentiousness of some of the early work are plain for all to see; but these faults are not paramount. The authority and the incisive rhetoric of 'Consider' established themselves from the start:

> Consider this and in our time
> As the hawk sees it or the helmeted airman:
> The clouds rift suddenly—look there
> At cigarette-end smouldering on a border
> At the first garden party of the year.
> Pass on, admire the view of the massif
> Through plate-glass windows of the Sport Hote
> Join there the insufficient units
> Dangerous, easy, in furs, in uniform,
> And constellated at reserved tables,
> Supplied with feelings by an efficient band,
> Relayed elsewhere to farmers and their dogs
> Sitting in kitchens in the stormy fens.

It is a panoptic, a magisterial view that Auden takes ('As the hawk sees it or the helmeted airman'), and it expects attention. It is at the same time self-confident, easy, and menacing; the tone is brisk and cool, and one can hear behind the lines Auden's voice as Spender described it: 'He would hold the vowels between the consonants as though in steel forceps.' It is (to use a favourite word of his at the time) 'clinical'. It is also a strange mixture of impressionism and analysis; the figurative details—clouds, cigarette-end, border, massif, plate-glass windows of the hotel, people sitting at tables in furs and uniforms, band, the placing of the farmers and their dogs in the last lines—all carry an impression of particularity mated with suggestive resonance. It has the concentration and clarity of the bird's-eye-view, and the distancing as well; but it suggests details beyond those it chooses to present.

This is one of the characteristic tones of Auden's early poems, but it is not the only one. There are poems that are hesitant, even perhaps deliberately stumbling, in their searching out of a statement:

> For what as easy
> For what though small,
> For what is well
> Because between,
> To you simply
> From me I mean . . .

Such lines have a runic or cryptic quality, a curious extension of Auden's interest in Old English poetry and in the Norse sagas (he was very conscious of his Norse descent), which could be seen as early as *Paid on Both Sides*. It is sometimes as if connections have purposely been rubbed out; and one knows from other sources (for example, Christopher Isherwood's account of Auden's undergraduate procedures in *Lions and Shadows*) that he occasionally made poems by constructing an amalgam of what he considered to be the best lines from poems which had otherwise been scrapped. But many more are straightforward, even narrative, in structure, in a way quite different from the work of T. S. Eliot that Auden and his contemporaries admired. Take the opening of 'Missing':

> From scars where kestrels hover,
> The leader looking over
> Into the happy valley,
> Orchard and curving river,

May turn away to see
The slow fastidious line
That disciplines the fell,
Hear curlew's creaking call
From angles unforeseen,
The drumming of a snipe
Surprise where driven sleet
Has scalded to the bone
And streams are acrid yet
To an unaccustomed lip; . . .

This, though characteristically Auden's, shares something with poets he admired before he discovered Eliot: Housman and Edward Thomas, two poets who have seldom, if ever, been called 'difficult'. And this is perhaps the point at which to establish one of the reasons that gave Auden a wide appeal from early days: that he was not impenetrably 'difficult', much of the time, for all his assured modernity, so that he was not the preserve simply of clever undergraduates and metropolitan intellectuals, but spoke equally—and eloquently—to provincial schoolboys, such as the young Roy Fuller (see Chapter Nine), who has written of the astonishing impact made on him by his first reading of Auden in the early 1930s. He was 'modern', he spoke of the time in which he lived, but he did not seem to presuppose (for example) an apparatus of polyglot scholarship such as *The Waste Land* appeared to present.

Much has been written about Auden as a political poet—even *the* political poet—of the 1930s; but in fact the direct political content of *Poems* (1930) and *Look, Stranger* (1936) is small. Even the strange 'English Study', *The Orators*, that appeared between these two books, for all the Marxist notions that have been read into it, is much more a work that has its roots in Jung, Groddeck and Layard—psychologists, prophets of the psyche rather than political analysts. It is a fantasy, a journal of personal obsessions too, which has a relationship with the grotesque and almost surrealist invented world of 'Mortmere'—that private country, or private joke, of Isherwood and Edward Upward, described by Isherwood in *Lions and Shadows*. It was not really until the late

1930s—in *Spain* (1937) and *Journey to a War* (1939)—that Auden
dealt in other than generalized terms with the political world;
and by that time he had shed whatever didactic partisan views he
may once have held. (I should perhaps mention *The Dance of
Death*, an early dramatic satire in light charade form: it is his most
consistently Marxist piece, in which Marx himself appears and
is seen at the end as a logically inevitable but also rather comic
figure.) No totally committed political animal could have written,
as Auden did in *Spain*, of 'the flat ephemeral pamphlet and the
boring meeting'; as for 'the necessary murder'—that notorious
phrase which enlisted the scorn of George Orwell, and which
Auden later somewhat neutralized to 'The conscious acceptance
of guilt in the fact of murder', before eventually abandoning the
whole poem—it has always seemed to me as much a piece of
role-playing as anything in *The Orators*: a rhetorical, schoolboy-
gang phrase. In this sense, Leavis is right about Auden's posture
as an arrested adolescent. But the 'In Time of War' sequence
(from *Journey to a War*) strikes no such attitudes: it has a distinct
detachment, even from events in that year when

> Austria died and China was forsaken,
> Shanghai in flames and Teruel retaken.

What the sequence looks for—and it is summed up in the 'Commentary' with which it ends—is that 'change of heart' forecast in
a poem several years before. In this 'Commentary', he concludes:

> Ruffle the perfect manners of the frozen heart,
> And once again compel it to be awkward and alive,
> To all it suffered once a weeping witness.
>
> Clear from the head the masses of impressive rubbish;
> Rally the lost and trembling forces of the will,
> Gather them up and let them loose upon the earth,
>
> Till they construct at last a human justice,
> The contribution of our star, within the shadow
> Of which uplifting, loving and constraining power
> All other reasons may rejoice and operate.

Such an injunction leads naturally towards the acceptance of
Christian teaching and Christian discipline which Auden found in

the early 1940s, and which some of his admirers found so discon-
certing (as happened, too, with those who were appalled or
contemptuous at Eliot's 'conversion' in 1927). The progression
can be seen as one that leads on without strain from Auden's
mind-healing preoccupations in the 1930s. The transition to *New
Year Letter* (1941) *is* a transition, not an entirely radical and unforeseen shift:

> That the orgulous spirit may while it can
> Conform to its temporal focus with praise,
>   Acknowledging the attributes of
>   One immortal, one infinite Substance;
>
> And the shabby structure of indolent flesh
> Give a resonant echo to the Word which was
>   From the beginning, and the shining
>   Light be comprehended by the darkness.

One does not need to be a convinced Christian to accept this;
what it does demand is the ability to make

> Another's moment of consent its own.

Renunciation and self-subjugation are allied to the sublimation to
which Auden had already, years earlier, paid allegiance in his
poem '1929'; in it, in 'death, death of the grain, our death', he
echoes both Eliot's 'This Birth was / Hard and bitter agony for us,
like Death, our death' ('Journey of the Magi') and, behind it, St
John's 'Except a corn of wheat fall into the ground and die, it
abideth alone: but if it die, it bringeth forth much fruit.' No
reader can sensibly persist in the notion that the 'pre-Christian'
and 'post-Christian' Audens are totally distinct creatures.

Perhaps a more frequent objection is that Auden's adoption of
the United States as his new home at the beginning of 1939
marked not only a rejection of his native country but the start of
a rapid decline in his poetry. Some critics would like to see the
episode as a dramatic break, a sloughing-off of Europe, and a
consequent lapsing into a cosy and languidly didactic style. Those
who had 'placed' Auden in the 1930s, and who had certain fixed
ideas about him, were disconcerted; some of their objections had

as much to do with an outraged sense of patriotism as anything else. In fact, Auden (together with his friend Christopher Isherwood) left for America in January 1939, a time when, it has been pointed out, the British government was asserting that the prospects for peace had never been brighter. So it was nothing to do with 'deserting the sinking ship' or escaping from danger: Auden had voluntarily faced danger in Spain in 1937 and in China in 1938.

But, quite apart from his motives, was there indeed a decline in his subsequent poetry? I think not. Almost to the end—and certainly up to *Epistle to a Godson* (1972)—there are poems in his successive books which can properly stand alongside his best earlier work. The title-poem of *The Shield of Achilles* (1955) has a classic inevitability:

> The mass and majesty of the world, all
> That carries weight and always weighs the same,
> Lay in the hands of others; they were small
> And could not hope for help, and no help came;
> What their foes liked to do was done; their shame
> Was all the worst could wish: they lost their pride
> And died as men before their bodies died.

In *About the House* (1966), there is Auden's elegy for Louis MacNeice, 'The Cave of Making', which is an equally authoritative pronouncement on his view of poetry itself:

> After all, it's rather a privilege
>   amid the affluent traffic
> to serve this unpopular art which cannot be turned into
>   background noise for study
> or hung as a status trophy by rising executives,
>   cannot be 'done' like Venice
> or abridged like Tolstoy, but stubbornly still insists upon
>   being read or ignored . . .

In *City Without Walls* (1969), 'Prologue at Sixty' is a self-elegy which combines, in the authentic Auden manner, high seriousness about important things with that lightness of tone which distinguished him from the beginning—that sardonic wit, sometimes even clownish, which so often combined with a note of

urgent warning or impending doom; one can see it in such poems
of the 1930s as 'Law Like Love', in many of the sonnets in his
sequence *The Quest*, in what he grouped together as 'Songs and
other musical pieces', and at its briskest and most amusing in
'Letter to Lord Byron', the long discursive poem which runs
through the book he worked on with MacNeice, *Letters from
Iceland* (1937). Finally, to mention one more late poem, 'An
Encounter' (in *Epistle to a Godson*) shows Auden's concise and
reverberant historical sense at work as perfectly as his *Spain*
almost thirty-five years earlier; the poem observes a meeting
between 'Attila and his Hun Horde' and Pope Leo by the River
Po in the year 452, and makes a telling point about the mysteries
of civilization and barbarism.

It could be said that Auden gradually became a sage and not a
prophet; but whichever function he took upon himself, he was
supremely an entertainer, a brilliant teacher and preacher, a
virtuoso who believed that poetry can display many voices, many
skills, and that it has something to do with the disinterested
intelligence—a view touched on in the lines from 'The Cave of
Making' quoted above. He was a prolific poet and (as one should
expect of a prolific poet—think of Wordsworth, Byron, Tennyson) some of his work is careless, coy, laborious, occasionally
boring. But the general level and impact of over forty years of
constant writing is exhilaratingly high. Along with Eliot, he has
been the most influential Anglo-American poet of the century,
and has been absorbed as well as imitated. One can say of Auden,
using his own words in his poem 'In Memory of W. B. Yeats':

> Now he is scattered among a hundred cities
> And wholly given over to unfamiliar affections,
> To find his happiness in another kind of wood
> And be punished under a foreign code of conscience;
> The words of a dead man
> Are modified in the guts of the living.

CHAPTER SEVEN

Louis MacNeice (1907–1963)
C. Day Lewis (1904–1972)
Stephen Spender (1909–)

The three poets with whom this chapter is concerned have always been associated with Auden in the public mind; all were born within a few years of one another, came from similar middle-class professional backgrounds, were contemporaries or near-contemporaries at Oxford after a public school education, and were all, in varying degrees of committedness, politically concerned in a direction which one can loosely call 'Left'. Roy Campbell, who vigorously despised them, lumped all four together as a composite figure in the 1930s—'MacSpaunday' (though he came to like MacNeice, which presumably accounts for the fact that later Campbell poems abuse 'Spaunday'). Auden certainly influenced his three contemporaries, but they should be looked at separately.

The viewpoints from which they started writing have been outlined by Stephen Spender in his autobiography, *World Within World*:

> Perhaps . . . the qualities which distinguished us from the writers of the previous decade lay not in ourselves, but in the events to which we reacted. These were unemployment, economic crisis, nascent fascism, approaching war . . .

From the literary point of view, the 1920–1930 decade in Britain looks unpolitical. Yet they were years of tremendous political upheaval and social change. In 1922, Mussolini came to power in Italy; in 1926 the General Strike paralysed Britain, and many feared a revolution; in 1929 there was the Wall Street crash and similar financial chaos in Europe during the early 1930s, resulting in widespread unemployment. Poets who had fought in the war and survived, such as Siegfried Sassoon, Edmund Blunden and Robert Graves, recoiled from any political activism. Edith Sitwell was, in the popular mind, the leader of the 1920s *avant garde* (far more so than Eliot), and her verbal and rhythmical fancies, such as *Façade*, took no notice of social matters. It was left to the generation slightly younger than the war poets, men whose childhood had been spent during the war, to face what was happening and to attempt a literature of protest and warning.

This was perhaps least so of Louis MacNeice. Though he was an observant 'social' poet, well aware of what was going on in the world of affairs, many of his best poems draw on the past, on common emotions, and on personal matters. Important in his personality was his feeling for his roots in Ireland, his memories of what he felt was in many ways a lonely and unhappy childhood, his training as a classical scholar, together with a delight in non-intellectual things (games, drink, food), and—most of all—the tug between the gregarious and genial man and the melancholy solitary. An early poem which effectively gives in miniature part of the essence of MacNeice is the lyric 'Snow', written in 1935. It is a poem that has been subjected to a good deal of footling and irrelevant analysis: twelve lines of apparent simplicity have brought the exegetes out in force. It is a sensuous poem—sight, taste, touch and hearing overlap in it—and it is also a poem about apprehension, multiplicity and quiddity, that 'instress' and 'inscape' of Hopkins:

> World is crazier and more of it than we think,
> Incorrigibly plural. I peel and portion
> A tangerine and spit the pips and feel
> The drunkenness of things being various.

And behind or beyond this variousness is an unarticulated sense of menace, of the 'otherness' of the world:

> There is more than glass between the snow and the huge roses.

'Snow' does all this lightly, teasingly, lyrically. And it is because MacNeice's tone was often apparently light (in a gayer and more insouciant way than Auden's) that he tended, right from the beginning, to be classified—indeed, patronized—as a light-weight, a journalist in verse. True, he packed a great deal of the paraphernalia of the modern world into his poems in a riot of imagery—buses, soda siphons, diabetes, Picasso, Dunlop tyres, golf, bank accounts, telephones, jet engines, factories, films, jazz. This wide range of snapshot modern reference is particularly apparent in his early 'eclogues'—modern versions of the classical and Renaissance dialogues between shepherds. In these, all the apparatus (and decay) of modern civilization are in the fore-ground. His love of brisk shock treatment can be seen in them, too; in 'An Eclogue for Christmas', for example, which begins

A. I meet you in an evil time.
B.   The evil bells
   Put out of our heads, I think, the thought of everything else.

Here all the stock associations of Christmas are meant to be shattered at the first blow. And the poem ends with an agnostic statement typical of MacNeice, in which all doubt and all belief are left open:

Goodbye to you, this day remember is Christmas, this morn
They say, interpret it your own way, Christ is born.

It was a basic agnosticism, doubtful of all dogmas, religious or political. Over twenty years after 'An Eclogue for Christmas', he wrote *Autumn Sequel*: Canto XXV ends

the skies are warning
That a new sun is rising and that now,
Take it what way you like, is really Christmas morning.

But both the reporting, the 'naming of things', and the shock tactics were part of a lively, observant mind that had its own depths and quirks. A key early poem is 'Turf-stacks', which dates from 1932. In it he looks nostalgically but without senti-mentality at the simple, and also onerous, life of the Irish peasantry, and contrasts with it other men's need 'of a fortress against ideas and against the / Shuddering insidious shock of the theory-vendors, / The little sardine men . . .' The urge to escape from dogmatists, doom-merchants, 'theory-vendors', to keep one's privacy, is there, again, in 'Memoranda for Horace', which dates from the last year of his life:

> . . . and yet today in London
> When all the loudspeakers bellow
> 'Wolf repeat Wolf!' I can find asylum
> As you did, either in language
> Or laughter or with the tangles.

In the thirty years that lie between these two poems, there is a whole range of forms, subjects, incidents and enthusiasms in MacNeice; but the central personality is the same—wry, angular, amused, watchful, a curious mixture of reticence and fluency, aware that nothing was simple or plain yet impatient with obfuscation and pretentiousness. He found his poetic voice, or voices, early. He went through a difficult period of about ten years (roughly, the mid-1940s until the mid-1950s), when he continued to be the prolific poet he always was but produced work which too often seemed to be both copious and strained. The work he did for the BBC, by which he was employed as a Features writer and producer for twenty years, may have had something to do with this, encouraging a tedious productivity and a hectic 'public' manner that did not suit him. But his last two books, *Solstices* (1961) and *The Burning Perch* (1963), contain poems as good as anything he wrote in the 1930s.

Among the favourite anthology pieces (and on the whole anthologists have chosen well from MacNeice) are 'The Sunlight on the Garden', the harshly exuberant 'Bagpipe Music', and 'Prayer Before Birth'. This last poem, technically one of his most adventurous, keeps an excellent balance between sentimentality and toughness. The shape of the poem is itself an expression of its theme—the slow, hesitant urging forth of the child from the womb. The internal rhymes and the repetitive syntax make it incantatory, the tone becoming more and more insistent, more and more desperate, as the rhythm becomes cumulative. Each section is carefully worked out, from the shunning of those creatures, real and imaginary, which terrify childhood, through

prayers against outer coercion and for inner light, through for-
giveness for delegated wrongdoing, through the final plea to

> rehearse me
> In the parts I must play and the cues I must take,

to the final prayer for individuality and freedom, without which
life is death: 'Otherwise kill me.'

But there are much later poems, in the last two books, which
deserve to be picked out in future anthologies: 'Charon' and
'Thalassa', with their dark stoicism, and the haunted nostalgia of
'Soap Suds' and 'Apple Blossom':

> For the last blossom is the first blossom
> And the first blossom is the best blossom
> And when from Eden we take our way
> The morning after is the first day.

Themes of childhood and nostalgia in these last poems are wedded
to forms and metres that often have something of the nursery
rhyme or the folk poem about them; and in 'Chateau Jackson' he
builds a whole mysteriously nihilistic *tour de force* on the structure
of the old verse about the house that Jack built. The idea of play
is strong in MacNeice, but it is always play with a purpose and
done to strict rules: this too is part of the child-world, as is the
emphasis on magic, the irrational and dreams. Since his death in
1963, MacNeice has come to seem the most interesting and impressive of the conventionally grouped 'Thirties poets', next in
stature to Auden and, like Auden, a poet who cannot be thought
of as confined to one particular decade.

C. DAY LEWIS

C. Day Lewis, who died in 1972 after a long illness, was probably
as prolific a writer as MacNeice, and his reputation went through
as many fluctuations. But he seems a less distinct poet. From the

beginning, he seemed to lean most heavily on the achievements of others. He began as a thoroughly unremarkable Georgian poet (in *Beechen Vigil*, 1925, and *Country Comets*, 1928). In *Transitional Poem, From Feathers to Iron* and *The Magnetic Mountain*, it was clear that he had adopted Auden as a mentor, and parts of these three long poems have some of Auden's most irritating early mannerisms, such as the false heartiness of lines like

> Then I'll hit the trail for that promising land;
> May catch up with Wystan and Rex my friend.

He was also, for a time, the most aggressively communist of the four, responsible for such lines (later suppressed by him, which is fair enough) as 'Why do we all, seeing a Red, feel small?' As for 'social comment' in general, the modernities look self-conscious. The poem 'You that love England', for example, aims didactically at a 'zero hour' of revolution; but the imagery is either too contrived and decorative (as in the first stanza, in which natural things are painfully stretched into musical analogies) or too determinedly documentary (as in the patronizing references to the weekend excursionists 'on tandem or on pillion' from the town, where one feels Day Lewis's remoteness from the working-class or lower-middle-class background he is trying to embrace in a comradely spirit).

There is a great deal of honest self-analysis in these Day Lewis poems of the 1930s, some lyricism that is sometimes sensuous, sometimes spare, and in two poems ('Flight to Australia' and 'The Nabara') an ambitious attempt to rescue the narrative poem from neglect. But throughout his career he seemed to respond too readily to the seductive voices of those poets he admired: after Auden, as he moved into the 1940s, there was increasingly an infatuation with Hardy and with Meredith. At the same time, his public concerns in his poetry were gradually replaced by private ones: love and lost love especially, themes common to Hardy and Meredith. But Day Lewis's generous and genial temperament tended to soften his mentors, making them diffuse and losing their defining edges. The result is a Hardy who has been rather sentimentalized and made mellifluous, without the crab-bedness and angularity—as in 'The Unwanted':

> Sure, from such warped beginnings
>   Nothing debonair
> Can come? But neither shame nor panic,   .
>   Drugs nor sharp despair
> Could uproot that untoward thing,
> That all too fierce and froward thing:
> Willy-nilly born it was, divinely formed and fair.

There is no doubt that Day Lewis had a taste for pastiche, and a good deal of talent for it, as one can see in Part Five of *An Italian Visit* (1953), which is a sequence of poems 'after' or 'in the manner of' five well-known poets: a deliberate poetic exercise, and the Hardy, the Yeats and the Auden are clever and amusing. Even such an attractive poem as 'Walking Away' (from *The Gate*, 1962) has a slightly blurred effect: in it, the poet remembers watching his son, now a grown man, walking away from him to school 'With the pathos of a half-fledged thing set free / Into a wilderness', and the detail in these first three stanzas is Hardy-esque. But the final stanza moralizes in a wistful way that sounds like diluted Robert Frost:

> I have had worse partings, but none that so
> Gnaws at my mind still. Perhaps it is roughly
> Saying what God alone could perfectly show—
> How selfhood begins with a walking away,
> And love is proved in the letting go.

The sincerity is moving, but the poem lacks the final assurance it should have because of the echoes, the uneasy awareness of high pastiche.

The 'occasional' pieces of his last years, celebrating dead friends and dead artists, rediscovering places, commemorating specific moments of pleasure and pain, have a sweetly lyrical, gently melancholy manner, and the general impression is a little too bland. The fact remains that Day Lewis's poems give, and continue to give, a good deal of pleasure to a large number of people, who perhaps find that emotional honesty and emotional simplicity of his kind, matched with graceful and rather obviously musical cadences, override more rigorous demands. The decent common-places of such a poem as 'The House where I was Born' illustrate this well:

> No one is alive to tell me
> In which of those rooms I was born,
> Or what my mother could see, looking out one April
> Morning, her agony done,
> Or if there were pigeons to answer my cooings
> From that tree to the left of the lawn.

STEPHEN SPENDER

Stephen Spender has shown in *World Within World* how, coming from a Victorian and Edwardian Liberal family of politicians and editors, he rebelled against that background but carried its rather muddled humanitarianism into his own unorthodox brand of communism. Yet his actual membership of the Communist Party lasted only a few months, for his sensitive and independent spirit could never be doctrinaire; he was always too willing, from the Party's point of view, to see both sides of the question, and too self-centred ever to be an adequate member of a revolutionary team.

A phrase of Louis MacNeice's about Spender as he saw him in the late 1920s—'redeeming the world by introspection'—could serve as an epigraph to the whole body of Spender's poetry as well. Indeed, it makes much better sense to look at the poems in this way, as attempts at redemptive and quasi-religious self-searching, than it does to see them as coming primarily from political or social concerns. Express trains, pylons, the unemployed at street corners, the burning of the Reichstag, or the Spanish Civil War—all these images were merely grit for Spender's insatiably self-regarding oyster.

He has always been (in his own words) 'an autobiographer

restlessly searching for forms in which to express the stages of my development'; or, in his 'Darkness and Light',

> To break out of the chaos of my darkness
> Into a lucid day, is all my will.

Self-absorption, self-revelation, turn their focus on weakness, impotence, the incapacity to act and, as a consequence, pity: these are all themes in Spender's first books, as they continue to be. What distinguishes the earlier work from the later is that the early poems, up to and including *The Still Centre* (1939), handle these elusive confessional themes with an instinctive firm skill, a sureness of cadence and phrasing that is entirely individual:

> What I expected was
> Thunder, fighting,
> Long struggles with men
> And climbing.
> After continual straining
> I should grow strong;
> Then the rocks would shake
> And I should rest long . . .
>
> He will watch the hawk with an indifferent eye
>   Or pitifully;
> Nor on those eagles that so feared him, now
>   Will strain his brow:
> Weapons men use, stone, sling and strong-thewed bow
>   He will not know.
> This aristocrat, superb of all instinct,
>   With death close linked
> Had paced the enormous cloud, almost had won
>   War on the sun;
> Till now, like Icarus mid-ocean-drowned,
>   Hands, wings, are found.

Admiration for the force and achievement of the perfected will, and for the hero figure who personifies that will, is tempered by equally romantic notions of the inevitability of failure, death, darkness: 'And all those other "I's" who long for "We dying".' The first-person of these early poems—and they are very much poems of the first-person—seems to be an amalgam of the majestic arch-creator, such as Beethoven ('What else is iron but he?'), and the slobbering scapegoat, such as Van Der Lubbe, accused by the Nazis of setting fire to the Reichstag ('I laugh because my laughter / Is like justice, twisted by a howitzer'). Later, his personal but also passive witness of the Spanish Civil War gave him a new focus for pity; in 'Ultima Ratio Regum', he says of a boy killed in the fighting,

> Ask. Was so much expenditure justified
> On the death of one so young and so silly
> Lying under the olive trees, O world, O death?

And in 'Two Armies' the actual combatants are seen as peaceful and innocent; it is only 'the furious words and minerals which destroy':

> Clean silence drops at night, when a little walk
> Divides the sleeping armies, each
> Huddled in linen woven by remote hands.
> When the machines are stilled, a common suffering
> Whitens the air with breath and makes both one
> As though these enemies slept in each other's arms.

In these poems, cloudy but passionate states of mind are fixed and defined with sensitive strokes. After that, in the poems he wrote during the Second World War and the small number since then, there seems a gradual loss of verbal conviction; the personality seems much the same, but it has somehow lost its lonely concentration. The introspection is still there but it redeems nothing: it seems fitful, distracted, a mood of perfunctory force, observing little, remembering less. At its best, Spender's early work gave almost purely personal impulses a firmer stamp and wider currency: something quite different from Day Lewis's moral emblems, and even more different from the hawk's-eye-view of Auden or the eclectic range of MacNeice.

CHAPTER EIGHT

Dylan Thomas (1914–1953)

Dylan Thomas's working life as a poet lasted a little over twenty years, but the most extraordinary thing about it was how much of the foundations were laid in a very short period towards the beginning. He was writing prolifically in his early teens, and when he was only seventeen he began work on some of the poems by which he is still remembered, such as the one that opens:

> Out of the sighs a little comes,
> But not of grief, for I have knocked down that
> Before the agony; the spirit grows,
> Forgets, and cries;
> A little comes, is tasted and found good . . .

Between 1931 and 1935, he drafted, and in many cases actually completed, most of his best poems. In other words, he had created something like the most significant body of his work by the age of twenty-one. He continued to draw on material from his adolescent notebooks well into the 1940s. There are a few later poems, such as 'Fern Hill' and 'Do Not Go Gentle Into That Good Night', that were not laid down at this early period, and which stand among his best. But the poems he was writing in his late adolescence established his main themes and his recognizable manner.

Thomas's first book, *Eighteen Poems*, was published when he was just twenty, in 1934. The themes are simple—sex, birth, death, and the fusion of these three. The speaker of the poems is frequently a child in the womb, or similar protomorphic being:

> Before I knocked and flesh let enter,
> With liquid hands tapped on the womb,
> I who was shapeless as the water
> That shaped the Jordan near my home
> Was brother to Mnetha's daughter
> And sister to the fathering worm.

> I who was deaf to spring and summer,
> Who knew not sun nor moon by name,
> Felt thud beneath my flesh's armour,
> As yet was in a molten form,
> The leaden stars, the rainy hammer
> Swung by my father from his dome.

These are stanzas from a poem which is a re-created 'memory' of life in the womb by a myth-figure who, in the last few lines, is seen as identified with Christ himself:

> You who bow down at cross and altar,
> Remember me and pity Him
> Who took my flesh and bone for armour
> And doublecrossed my mother's womb.

The word-play in 'doublecrossed' is typical: the protagonist in the poem is seen as literally crossing the womb twice, first as his own self-begetter and then as the child itself (Christ is both the Son of God and God himself); and the womb is 'doublecrossed' (tricked or cheated) because it is made to bring forth beings who die.

These poems begin with the assumption or insistence that we start to die from the moment we are born—even, indeed, from the moment we are conceived. And this continual process of dying links us with everything else in the world: the death of a flower comes under the same edict and force as our own death, because the powers of destruction are one. This is the whole burden of one of his best-known early poems, of which the following is the first stanza:

> The force that through the green fuse drives the flower
> Drives my green age; that blasts the roots of trees
> Is my destroyer.
> And I am dumb to tell the crooked rose
> My youth is bent by the same wintry fever.

The method (and it continued to be his method in most of his poems) can be seen fascinatingly in Thomas's work-sheets, many of which have been published: words are listed for their sound-properties, and are concentratedly and densely worked into hermetic, hypnotic rhythms, with the steady beat of the iambic pentameter as their ground bass. The thread of prose meaning, of paraphrasable content, is usually simple; what is sometimes difficult is their thickly clotted verbal texture.

It was at one time assumed that Thomas was a complete naif or primitive but, though he left school at the age of sixteen, it was Swansea Grammar School he attended, where his father was senior English master, and he came from a bookish home. He was widely read, despite all the tales about his taste for cowboy stories and children's comics. Certainly he read Yeats, Eliot and Auden while he was writing the poems of his adolescence, though they left few traces on his work: more importantly he must have read the poems of Hopkins and the prose of James Joyce, and stylistic mannerisms of these two can be found in much of Dylan Thomas. But it is true that he was not intellectually curious; he had a narrow, instinctive, original talent at which he worked intensely—at least, until his self-destructive impulses began to be augmented by the distractions of earning a living and keeping a family, the seductive pleasures of friends, congenial parasites and drink, and a generally evasive way of life.

A few of the early poems have a cryptic plainness or a plain rhetoric: for example, 'The hand that signed the paper' and 'And death shall have no dominion' (both of them in his second book, *Twenty-Five Poems*, published in 1936, though they were drafted in 1933 and could have appeared in his first book). 'The hand that signed the paper' is almost a metaphysical conceit on the subject of power:

> A hand rules pity as a hand rules heaven;
> Hands have no tears to flow.

If this reminds one of Herbert, then 'And death shall have no dominion' is equally likely to sound like a variation on Donne's sonnet 'Death, be not proud'. But they are not literary exercises and, though Thomas later tended to be humorously dismissive about the early poems (the work of 'a boily boy'), he continued to read them aloud in the recitals that made him famous. 'And death shall have no dominion' shows a characteristic and continuing Thomas trick, of verbal transference: e.g., 'the man in the wind and the west moon', where the eye or ear expect 'the man in the moon and the west wind'. Elsewhere in *Twenty-Five Poems* the congestion makes the rhetoric monotonous, as in the 'Altarwise by Owl-Light' sequence of sonnets, written in 1935, of which these are the first six lines:

> Altarwise by owl-light in the half-way house
> The gentleman lay graveward with his furies;
> Abaddon in the hangnail cracked from Adam,
> And, from his fork, a dog among the fairies,
> The atlas-eater with a jaw for news,
> Bit out the mandrake with to-morrow's scream.

It was in his third book, *The Map of Love* (1939), that Thomas included

> the only poem I ever wrote directly about the life and death of one particular human being I knew—and not about the very many lives and deaths, whether seen, as in my first poems, in the tumultuous world of my own being or, as in the later poems, in war, grief, and the great holes and corners of universal love.

This poem is 'After the Funeral'; as often, an early draft goes back as far as 1933, but in this case Thomas worked on it so thoroughly that five years later it was a new poem. It is an elegy for the old aunt with whom Thomas used to spend many of his holidays in rural Wales when he was a child. Ann Jones appears in one of the stories ('The Peaches') in his book of semi-autobiographical pieces, *Portrait of the Artist as a Young Dog*, where she is described as 'a little, brown-skinned, toothless, hunchbacked woman with a cracked, sing-song voice'. Not only is Ann (or Annie, as she is called in the story) described, but also the room in her cottage which, with its ferns and stuffed fox, is the setting of the poem. The poem therefore has a closely particularized relation to Thomas's personal life, and this is rare in his poetry.

'After the Funeral' can be divided into three parts—the funeral and funeral-feast; the bard's disclaimer; and the celebration or 'keen' over Ann's memory. The poem begins with an impressionistic picture of the funeral, with its donkey-like braying over the dead body, its ostentatious sorrow and ritualistic mourning; against this is set the

> muffle-toed tap
> Tap happily of one peg in the thick
> Grave's foot

as the earth is thrown back on to the coffin. The noise of the spade shakes the poet back to his memories of Ann when he was a child, and he 'slits his throat' in the gesture children use when they make a solemn and deadly promise; his promise is that he will never forget her. He is too moved to weep; he 'sheds dry leaves' whereas the mourners are openly snivelling into their sleeves, wiping the tears away. He stands alone in the room he remembers from his childhood, 'a room with a stuffed fox and a stale fern', and remembers also Ann's kindness, which was like a hidden fountain, nourishing all who came in contact with her in the 'parched worlds of Wales'.

Then the poet considers that such an image is too fulsome and wordy to please her spirit; she does not need a druid or bardic priest to pronounce a histrionic oration over her. Instead, he calls on nature to celebrate her love and her 'bent spirit'; the funeral is thus transferred in the poet's mind to the natural world, where her own natural virtue is the bell which calls the people to church, where the church itself is made by the trees bowing down (both in homage and to make an arch above her—in 'the ferned and foxy woods', which give a link with the dead fox and fern in the house) and where the church's cross is formed by four birds flying in the sky above. Now that she is dead, she goes through a creative metamorphosis in his mind; the humble flesh becomes a huge statue in memory of her, and though he knows that her real hands, voice and mind are now still, her strong little face twisted from the pain in which she died, she has become a monument, 'seventy years of stone'. Let these monuments of her body and spirit inspire him, he says, so that even the dead fox will be reborn and the dead fern create new life.

The method of 'After the Funeral' is one of reconciling contradictions and oppositions, and here it is useful to quote one of Thomas's statements on his own poetry—a rationalization of how he worked, and not wholly applicable to all his poems, but relevant in this case:

> A poem by myself needs a host of images, because its centre is a host of images. I make one image—though 'make' is not the word; I let, perhaps, an image be 'made' emotionally in me and then apply to it what intellectual and critical forces I possess; let it breed another, let that image contradict the first; make of the third image, bred out of the other two together, a fourth contradictory image, and let them all, within my imposed formal limits, conflict . . . The life in any poem of mine cannot move concentrically round a central image, the life must come out of the centre; an image must be born and die in another; and any sequence of my images must be a sequence of creations, re-creations, destructions, contradictions . . .

The main images on which this poem turns are (a) the fox and the fern, and (b) the real remembered Ann and the Ann whom the poet creates in his mind, 'a monstrous image blindly magnified out of praise'. These images are expanded, re-created, and reconciled. The fox and the fern are objects in the stuffy, dead room of the dead woman—representations of that stuffiness and deadness. The word 'stuffed' as applied to the fox is not only literal; it also carries the associations of its semi-homonym 'stuffy', and the funeral feast becomes 'the feast of tear-stuffed time'—the neighbours' and relatives' mourning is full of tears just as the fox (like the old woman) is full of age. The dead woman is juxtaposed with the dead fox which was her lifetime companion. Later, however, the fox and fern are transferred to their natural habitat, the wood which becomes (in the poet's mind) Ann's chapel. And in the end both are seen as representing the dead which might be brought to life by Ann's love.

The real Ann is a simple countrywoman, worn out by hard work, wasted by disease, hunchbacked, wizened, kind. Set against her is the monument which the 'bard' (the poet himself) carves for her; and there is a contrast between 'her flesh was meek as milk' and 'this skyward statue', between 'her scrubbed and sour humble hands' and 'These cloud-sopped, marble hands'. The poem itself becomes a monument.

I have concentrated on 'After the Funeral' because it makes a more coherent impression than many of Thomas's other poems, and because it illustrates so well his general method. His last book of poems (before his collected volume in 1952), *Deaths and Entrances*, includes a number which deal with 'war, grief, and the great holes and corners of universal love', poems such as 'A Refusal to Mourn the Death, by Fire, of a Child in London', 'Ceremony after a Fire Raid', and 'Dawn Raid'. But there are also several which draw on his nostalgia for childhood and thus have a link with 'After the Funeral': these are 'The Hunchback in the Park', 'Poem in October', 'Poem on his birthday' and 'Fern Hill'. In these poems, as in Vaughan, Traherne and Wordsworth, childhood is seen as a state of absolute innocence and grace from which man declines through the years. The child is involved in the process of time, and hence of death, though he does not know it:

> And nothing I cared, at my sky blue trades, that time allows
> In all his tuneful turning so few and such morning songs
>   Before the children green and golden
>   Follow him out of grace . . .
> Oh as I was young and easy in the mercy of his means,
>   Time held me green and dying
>   Though I sang in my chains like the sea.

And there are moments in adult life when that childhood suddenly becomes real again. In particular, birthdays remind the man of the child he once was; and both 'Poem in October' and 'Poem on his birthday' turn on this idea, the first at the age of thirty and the second at thirty-five. As in the early poems, life moves towards death, and so in 'Poem in October' (my italics)

> It was my thirtieth year *to heaven*
> Woke to my hearing . . .

It is a more wistful, less fiercely pessimistic, development of the theme of so many of his earlier poems:

> In the groin of the natural doorway I crouched like a tailor
> Sewing a shroud for a journey
> By the light of the meat-eating sun.

With a few exceptions, the last poems have, in their movement and language, an expansive, almost improvised air; they lack the tautness and strongly deliberate rhythms of *Eighteen Poems* and *Twenty-Five Poems*, and are in fact much closer in technique to his prose in *Portrait of the Artist as a Young Dog* and in his unfinished novel, *Adventures in the Skin Trade*, as well as in his radio 'play for voices', *Under Milk Wood*, though the poems do not attempt the fanciful humour of these. Carelessness of language (for example, the way the word 'lovely' is used in 'Fern Hill') is sometimes oddly mismatched with pointless elaboration of stanza forms, as in the 'Prologue' he wrote specially for the 1952 *Collected Poems*, in which the first of the 102 lines rhymes with the last, and so on inversely. It is as if the withdrawal of Thomas's inspiration brought with it a desperately frenetic drumming-up of spurious energy, which may be the explanation for the geometric contortions of 'Vision and Prayer' (in which half the stanzas are lozenge-shaped and half are hourglasses) and the verbose over-extension of 'A Winter's Tale', 'In Country Sleep', 'In the White Giant's Thigh' and 'Over Sir John's Hill'. Periodically and increasingly, he had gone through barren patches, commemorated as early as September 1938, when he wrote:

> On no work of words now for three lean months in the bloody
> Belly of the rich year and the big purse of my body
> I bitterly take to task my poverty and craft . . .

By the 1940s, though, it was not a matter of months but of years.

An exception is the elegy he wrote for his dying father in 1951, 'Do not go gentle into that good night'. Here the strictness of the villanelle form, with its metrical steadiness and its repeated lines and rhymes, imposes a solemn gravity:

> And you, my father, there on the sad height,
> Curse, bless, me now with your fierce tears, I pray.
> Do not go gentle into that good night.
> Rage, rage against the dying of the light.

A further elegy for his father, which was left unfinished at Thomas's own death in 1953, has the same simple strictness of form.

The 'legend' of Dylan Thomas has hindered more than it has helped. The journalists' headlines ('The poet they called a dangerous cherub', 'The Most Fantastic Character of Our Time'), the reminiscences and sycophantic memorializing of the 'I Knew Dylan' variety, the huge apparatus of pseudo-commentary and ponderous exegesis that has grown up round the man and his work—these should not, but often do, stand in the way between the reader and the finest achievements of this narrow but intense, strange and eloquent poet. The richness and resonance of the poems ideally suited his own reading at its, and their, best: of the many recordings, it is worth noticing how much better are those made in studios for the BBC and other broadcasting organizations than those which were made in public halls and auditoriums during his tours of the United States (he made three visits to give readings, and died during the final one), when he was too often tempted to bellow even his quieter poems. The studio readings have an inwardness and intimacy he could manage perfectly.

Despite all the maudlin references to his youth in the death-notices and reminiscences, one should remember that Thomas was thirty-nine when he died; almost exactly the same age as Wyatt, Herbert and Byron, and considerably older than Marlowe, Keats, Shelley and Wilfred Owen. There is a substantial body of work to consider: the 1952 *Collected Poems* can be looked at as a whole, and not simply as the unfinished foundations of a building. Looking at *The Poems* of 1971 (which add over a hundred more poems, almost all of them written between the ages of twelve and nineteen), it is arguable that he would have written very little more, except in the direction *Under Milk Wood* was taking him; and that particular vein was likely to be worked out soon. He managed in his poems at least a dozen times (some readers would put the figure much higher than that) to triumph against all the odds and produce work which is in the best canon of poetry in English. And that is more important than any talk of dangerous cherubs or fantastic characters.

CHAPTER NINE

Some Other Poets of the 1930s and 1940s

Though the decade of the 1930s is often seen as the Age of Auden, dominated entirely by him and the triumvirate of MacNeice, Day Lewis and Spender, literary history is never quite so neat. Within a very few years of the publication of Auden's first book, Dylan Thomas published his *18 Poems*, George Barker his *Thirty Preliminary Poems*, and David Gascoyne his *Roman Balcony*—all of them first books which had little or nothing to do with the concerns and manners of Auden. John Betjeman was a contemporary of Auden's at Oxford, but his own first book, *Mount Zion*, published in 1931, was as distinctly 'Betjemanesque' as anything he has written since. And other poets, slightly older, such as Roy Campbell and Stevie Smith, were working their own individual plots of ground throughout the 1930s. In this chapter I want to look at the poetry of these six, and at others who began writing in the Thirties and the war years, though in some cases their reputations have taken longer to establish. I also want to discuss four poets who were killed during the Second World War while they were still in their early twenties.

Roy Campbell's poetic personality was vigorous, masculine and prolific. Born in South Africa, where he raged against the philistinism and provincialism of the country, he became something of a deliberate philistine himself when he came to England, and raged equally fiercely against what he considered to be the effeminacy and inbred cosiness of English literary life. As a Roman Catholic and an almost Yeatsian believer in 'nobility' and 'aristocracy', he was one of the few writers in Britain to support Franco's cause during the Spanish Civil War, and the only one actually to fight on Franco's side. 'The Georgiad', a satire on English literary personalities of the early 1930s, made him one set

of enemies, and such lyrics as 'Hot Rifles' and 'Christ in Uniform'
—seeing the war in Spain as a holy crusade against the infidel—
made him another. Yet he was so open in his combativeness, so
almost child-like in his hates and enthusiasms, that his satire
hardly ever seems sour or rancorous.

He was technically inventive, though always working in
traditional forms. His lyrics are full of verbal zest, especially
when he could spread himself, in such an extended lyric as 'The
Palm'; and he had a Byronic eloquence (the Byron of 'Childe
Harold' rather than 'Don Juan') in such rhetorical poems as
'Tristan da Cunha'. Sometimes his metres are too rollicking, his
rhymes over-ingenious and unintentionally comic, his exuberance too exhausting; but his epigrams are neat and contemptuously biting, and show none of these faults. The one 'On Some
South African Novelists' has gained currency far beyond its
ostensible subject-matter:

> You praise the firm restraint with which they write—
> I'm with you there, of course:
> They use the snaffle and the curb all right,
> But where's the bloody horse?

Of all Campbell's work, some of these epigrams have survived
best, together with a handful of lyrics and some of the fine trans-
lations from St John of the Cross and Baudelaire.

George Barker, like his contemporary Dylan Thomas, had a
precocious start. In the 1930s and 1940s, he was seen to be as
promising and interesting as Thomas. It was Barker, not Thomas,
who was picked out by Yeats for inclusion in the *Oxford Book of
Modern Verse* (1936)—the youngest poet in that anthology.
Francis Scarfe's book *Auden and After*, which gives a fair picture
of critical orthodoxies in the early 1940s, gave equal prominence
to Barker and Thomas. But since Dylan Thomas's death in 1953
there has been no doubt which of the two poets has had greater
attention and praise. In the past twenty-odd years, Barker has
seemed to be judged as if he lay in the shadow of Thomas's
fame.

This is a pity, because throughout his career Barker's best

poems have been striking and powerful. His best books are probably *Lament and Triumph* (1940) and *Eros in Dogma* (1944), but there are magnificent things in all of them—as well as the faults of prolixity, verbal and rhythmical ludicrousness, tasteless rhetoric and stupendous clumsiness that have marked much of his output from the beginning until now. Barker himself is aware of all the common-sensical objections:

> Personally I have never been on the side of the angelic perfectionists. I believe that perfect poetry is no more possible than perfect people. And I believe that if you have got to make mistakes you might as well make great mistakes, because these will at least show other people what not to do . . . When Shakespeare put down the pen and died he had committed a hundred and one mistakes of excess and commission, but he had also discovered the English language.

Such poems as his 'Elegy on Spain', written in 1939 and inspired by seeing a photograph of a child killed in an air raid on Barcelona, give a picture of appalled reaction quite different from the Civil War poems of Auden, Spender, or of course Roy Campbell:

> O ecstatic is this head of five year joy:
> Captured its butterfly rapture on a paper:
> And not the rupture of the right eye may
> Make any less this prettier than a picture.
> O now, my minor moon, dead as meat
> Slapped on a negative's plate, I hold
> The crime of the bloody time in my hand.

Barker's most ambitious effort has been 'The True Confession of George Barker', the first part of which appeared in 1950 but which was not published in its complete form until 1965. The anguished and majestic rhetoric of some of its sections is like nothing else in modern English poetry:

> I know only that the heart
> Doubting every real thing else
> Does not doubt the voice that tells
> Us that we suffer. The hard part
> At the dead centre of the soul
> Is an age of frozen grief
> No vernal equinox of relief
> Can mitigate, and no love console.

Barker continues, as he has always done, to take great risks within the romantic convention of the poet as divine scapegoat, but the assured seriousness of this stance, together with his eloquent gifts, more often achieve success than he is nowadays given credit for.

David Gascoyne was even more precocious than Dylan Thomas or George Barker: he was sixteen when *Roman Balcony* was published, and in the next few years brought out a novel, another book of poems, and a survey of surrealism. Surrealism (the anti-rational literary and artistic movement which developed in France and Central Europe during the 1920s) never became really at home in England; but Gascoyne—who was at one time called 'the only whole-hearted English Surrealist'—enthusiastically adopted it in his very early days. By the time he was twenty-two, however, he had moved away from writing in this automatic manner. He began to write a sequence of religious poems, called 'Miserere', all of which are concerned with the spiritual desolation of those who are banished—and know they are banished—from the sight of God: a facet of Gerard Manley Hopkins's explorations, but handled very differently from Hopkins, with a fine-drawn austerity:

> Here am I now cast down
> Beneath the black glare of a netherworld's
> Dead suns, dust in my mouth, among
> Dun tiers no tears refresh: am cast
> Down by a lofty hand . . .

There has been little work of this quality by Gascoyne since 'Miserere', but 'A Wartime Dawn', written a few years later, is a haunting poem, in which every sense seems strained with apprehension, and bears out the description of Gascoyne's poetry as being like the journal of a sensitive invalid:

> Nearest within the window's sight, ash-pale
> Against a cinder coloured wall, the white
> Pearblossom hovers like a stare . . .
> A pang of poignant odour from the earth, an unheard sigh
> Pregnant with sap's sweet tang and raw soil's fine
> Aroma, smell of stone, and acrid breath
> Of gravel puddles . . .

With John Betjeman, the difficulty may be to detach him from his popularity—a popularity which has made some people suspicious of his work. His *Collected Poems*, first published in 1958 after a succession of slim volumes during the previous quarter-century, quickly reached sales which its publishers were happy to compare to Byron's. His work by no means appeals exclusively to the 'upper-middle-class and lower-middle-aged' public characterized as such by some derogatory commentator. Both Auden and Larkin have praised him, and one can see why: Auden recognized the versatile technical skill, Larkin the 'dramatic urgency' that springs from 'what he really feels about real life'. It is true that his most frequently quoted poems are those, such as 'A Subaltern's Love-song' ('Miss Joan Hunter Dunn, Miss Joan Hunter Dunn'), which are gently absurd essays in light verse, making fun of certain English attitudes, while at the same time appearing to share so many of those attitudes that the poet's own stance is sometimes a little uncertain. But there is an altogether more astringent side to Betjeman, in which nostalgia, fear, hard-won faith and simple goodness contend, and a basic melancholy —as in 'NW5 & N6', in which the careful and circumstantial re-creation of childhood, of a sadistic nurse imposing her puritan will in the midst of outwardly cosy suburbia, moves to its blank and bleak conclusion:

> 'World without end'. It was not what she'ld do
> That frightened me so much as did her fear
> And guilt at endlessness. I caught them too,
> Hating to think of sphere succeeding sphere
> Into eternity and God's dread will
> I caught her terror then. I have it still.

The easy surfaces, lyrical measures or ambling pedestrianism of Betjeman's poetry move above areas of experience which are not simple at all, and which had no proper voice until he gave them one: Victorian churches, railway stations, brand names, provincial backwaters—these are things about which he is at once deft, light and serious. His most sustained effort so far has been *Summoned By Bells* (1960), the verse autobiography which takes him from childhood to going down dimly and regretfully from

Oxford. Written mainly in correct but conversational blank verse, interspersed with the hymn-like rhyming stanzas he has often used elsewhere, the poem is full of what Betjeman himself has called 'rapid changes of mood and subject', so that it comprehends a whole complex growing personality, amusingly, gravely, accurately.

Stevie Smith, who died in 1971, was as much an original as John Betjeman. When she first tried to publish her poems in the 1930s she found little enthusiasm for them (her first book was a novel, *Novel on Yellow Paper*, published in 1936, a year before her first volume of poems); her odd mixture of whimsical gloom, eccentric common sense, incantation, nursery-rhyme, doggerel and knowingness was an acquired taste. Gradually she came to be recognized as a very special poet of strangeness, loneliness and quirky humour, particularly with her *Selected Poems* of 1962 and the Penguin selection published in the same year. She often made poems out of fancies and imaginings which might have seemed to anyone else unpromising and quite unpoetic, such as the lines:

> Do take Muriel out
> She is looking so glum
> Do take Muriel out
> All her friends have gone . . .
>
> Do take Muriel out
> Although your name is Death . . .

She was always a poet concerned with death, and during her last years it had been her central theme—not really gloomy, but seen in an almost sprightly way—death as something to be comfortably welcomed, like a neighbour:

> I have a friend
> At the end
> Of the world.
> His name is a breath
>
> Of fresh air.
> He is dressed in
> Grey chiffon. At least
> I think it is chiffon.
> It has a
> Peculiar look, like smoke.

She could sustain a narrative (as in 'Angel Boley'), indulge in sly theological polemics ('How do you see the Holy Spirit of God?'), be bewilderingly whimsical ('Mrs Blow and Her Animals') or quietly poignant ('Oblivion'), and she had an offhand and mocking humour. Her blend of levity, loneliness, and sometimes asperity, was inimitable.

Roy Fuller's poems began to appear during the 1930s, in such magazines as Geoffrey Grigson's *New Verse*. They had a pretty strong taste of Auden about them, and were witty, intelligent, rather dry, very much aware of what was going on in the political world round him but having a wry detachment as well. Though he went on to write better poems than these, such qualities still hold good in Fuller's work. Some of the poems he wrote on naval service during the Second World War, such as 'The Green Hills of Africa', 'The Giraffes' and 'The Middle of a War', have a well-judged eloquence which, in the immediately post-war period, he seemed deliberately to drop, in favour of a low-keyed colloquialism, exemplified in such openings as these:

> Reading the shorthand on a barber's sheet
> In a warm and chromium basement in Cannon Street . . .

> After a night of insomnia I read
> In the morning paper of the death of Gide . . .

> On the aeroplane from Nice I lost my pen
> That instrument of poetry and affairs.

One began to be aware in the 1950s that he was not simply a good 'reporter of experience', with such poems as 'The Ides of March', in which his capacity for rich and developed thinking-aloud became apparent, and a technical ability which showed itself in a whole range of forms working out a shaping and phrase-making imagination. His *Collected Poems* of 1962, drawing on work that went back to the 1930s, confirmed his standing, and he has gone on through the 1960s and 1970s with a striking succession of books, of which the best is probably *New Poems* (1968); here his strict forms and ingenious rhymes were largely jettisoned and the voice became deceptively relaxed, allowing moments of blankness or self-disgust or facetiousness to be caught, entirely without straining pose or frigid distancing—then moving to something graver and more elevated. An example is 'Romance', which begins with the disarmingly snobbish mock-rhetorical flourish of

> Girl with fat legs, reading Georgette Heyer,
> Shall I arrange you in my pantheon?

But this ends with these lines:

> Return, great goddesses, and your society
> Where even little girls develop
> Strong superegos, and the misfortune
> Of woman's weak moral nature is unknown;
> And the wars are waged on a lower epicycle
> By armour diminutive as stag-beetles;
> And poets forbidden to sing of their diseases
> Or amatory botherations;
> And only with end-stopped irony.

Without being academic, Fuller is an alert, very widely read, endlessly curious and unashamedly intellectual poet. More than any poet since Auden, he has used his reading of Freud and Jung (and Marx too) in trying to make sense of human drives and infirmities, and he has a strong sense of history.

Gavin Ewart was also a precocious arrival in the pages of Grigson's magazine *New Verse*, having his first poem published there in 1933 when he was only sixteen. Like Roy Fuller, he had obviously learned a lot from Auden, and sometimes the results looked like pastiche as well as parody—'Audenesque for an Initiation' falls somewhere between the two. But after the 1930s there was silence, only sporadically interrupted, for over twenty years, until a succession of Ewart poems began to appear in the early Sixties. The odd thing was that the new Ewart turned out to be a recognizable version of the old, though with a blacker and more 'permissive' humour—a sign of changed times rather than changed personalities, perhaps. As an entertainer and satirist, enjoying technical trickery and loathing all portentous and self-important poetry, resolutely determined to present things-as-they-are and not things-as-people-pretend-they-are, Ewart has gone from strength to strength. But he is not only a joker—though he is often a good one; he also deals with what he has called 'the pressures and pleasures of contemporary urban life'? with a mordant awareness of the unpleasant ironies. The attractive and disdainful accuracy of some of these Ewart poems sometimes reminds one of MacNeice, as in the touching conclusion to 'If', a love poem that is serious without solemnity, and in which the earlier jokes are part of the whole, not mere decorations stuck in because of unease:

> That pub still stands, where I celebrated my affinity
> with you; and its trade doesn't slacken;
> and the long line of lovers stretches to infinity
> in the bed-sitting-room and in the bracken,
> and in that walled courtyard with its trees
> you and I are the ghostly absentees.

I must briefly mention some of the poets whose apparent promise was cut off by their deaths in the Second World War: Alun Lewis, Sidney Keyes, Keith Douglas and Drummond Allison. Only one of them—Douglas—has a reputation that stands in any way on 'war' poems; the nature of the Second World War campaigns, and the change in national consciousness, meant that there was no equivalent figure to Wilfred Owen, or even to Sassoon, in the 1939–45 period. Alun Lewis, dead at twenty-nine, was already a formed human being, feeling his way as a poet from a sensuous lyricism and an awareness of what Edward Thomas's work had to teach him towards something that he never quite made his own. His rich descriptiveness, tenderness, compassion, are plain in many poems. Sidney Keyes was at the time of his death in 1942 acclaimed as the best of the 'war poets', and the feeling persisted for some time afterwards, but his work has not lasted well. The neo-romantic atmosphere in which he began to write, which was popular in the wartime Oxford where he was educated, allowed him to develop some of his worst faults—straining for effect, literariness, and a pervasive sense of everything being at several exalted removes from life. But there are some memorably plangent lines:

> A foreign corpse with blue-rimmed eyes, and limbs
> Drawn limp and racked between the jigging waves . . .
>
> I am in love with all those who have entered
> The night that smells of petals and of dust.

Keith Douglas had the most unsettled and unsettling talent of these four. In some ways an aggressive, extrovert character, he had a dark, self-destructive side to him as well, and the conflict is there in the poems: 'Remember me when I am dead, and simplify me when I'm dead' one of his poems sardonically begins. The landscape of the Western Desert is very much part of his later poems, apparent in 'Words':

> For instance this stooping man, the bones of whose face are
> like the hollow birds' bones, is a trap for words.
> And the pockmarked house bleached by the glare
> whose insides war has dried out like gourds
> attracts words . . .

Drummond Allison seems equally complex and contradictory, and is still the least known of the most interesting English poets killed in the war. Within his briskly organized intellectual framework, he had a vein of fantasy which produced some excellent poems, such as 'The Brass Horse', of which this is the first stanza:

> Never presume that in this marble stable
> Furnished with imitation stalactites,
> Witheld from any manger and unable
> To stamp impatient hooves or show the whites
> Of eyes whose lids are fixed, on sulky nights
> He asks himself no questions, has no doubt
> What he a brazen engine is about.

Of other poets who grew up in the 1930s, served in the war, but survived, Charles Causley is one of the most attractive. Although his first collection was not published until 1951, he began writing during the war when he was in the navy, and the sea is still often present in his work. The sea-shanty, the ballad, the jaunty narrative have always been his forms, outwardly simple, often humorous, always bright and melodious. But his

range has widened and deepened since such racy exercises as
'Cowboy Song':

> I come from Salem County
>   Where the silver melons grow,
>   Where the wheat is sweet as an angel's feet
>   And the zithering zephyrs blow . . .

He is not, in fact, the simple old-fashioned lyrical soul some
people take him to be. In 'Ballad of the Bread Man', for instance,
the lively step of the verse is quite clearly and deliberately working against what it is actually saying, and the contrast is a large
part of the effect:

> Mary stood in the kitchen
> Baking a loaf of bread.
> An angel flew in through the window.
> We've a job for you, he said.

Even when the verse is reduced to something very like doggerel,
as in 'I Saw a Jolly Hunter', the effect is a sophisticated one, calling
on memories of nursery rhymes to give the poem irony. And
Causley has a grander, more measured manner too, often drawing on the personal and circumstantial, with the old lyrical
sweetness but with new depths, as in the conclusion to 'Con-
ducting a Children's Choir':

> I bait the snapping breath, curled claw, the deep
> And delicate tongue that lends no man its aid.
> The children their unsmiling kingdoms keep,
> And I walk with them, and I am afraid.

There is in fact a great deal more art in Causley's work than may
appear at first sight. In immediate impact, entertaining speak-
ability, comic attack and even in social comment, he is much
superior to the 'pop' poets (see Chapter Twelve) who use some
of the same themes and who may seem to have some of the same
appeal. 'Reservoir Street', 'Demolition Order', 'Devonport' and
'Hospital' have a gritty basis of realism, and 'The Visit' a per-
sistence of observation and a finely controlled contempt that
show ambitious areas into which Causley is penetrating.

A proper roll-call—even a selective one—of good poets who began writing in the 1930s and 1940s would probably have to include at least ten or a dozen others: Norman Cameron, Lawrence Durrell, Laurie Lee, Norman MacCaig, Norman Nicholson, F. T. Prince, Henry Reed, Anne Ridler, Bernard Spencer . . . But such listing quickly becomes fatuous, a mere assurance that the author is decently omniscient; and a guide or primer is no place in which to display that.

CHAPTER TEN

Robert Graves (1895–   )
William Empson (1906–   )
Edwin Muir (1887–1959)

In his autobiography, *Goodbye to All That*, written when he was thirty-three, Robert Graves presented himself as someone who had crammed into a brief space more extremes and oddities of experience than most people undergo in a long lifetime. He made a vow at the age of fifteen never to compromise himself in his vocation as a poet; and, though he has been a prolific writer in many different directions since the 1920s, his chief reputation has been as a poet. It is a reputation that stands on the subtly individual flavour of his work, and on its remarkable unbroken continuity, not on innovation. Though one can find traces of Graves's influence in many poets (and poets of disparate sorts), he has always been too quirky and isolated, too much his own man, to have had a keen following of dogmatic disciples.

He published his early poems during the First World War (in which he fought as an infantry officer, and indeed was reported officially dead of wounds on his twenty-first birthday), and in his successive volumes of collected poems he has continued to republish some of them—for example, 'In the Wilderness', concerned with Christ's fasting in the desert and written in a short-lined, irregularly rhymed style influenced by an early Graves master, John Skelton, the late medieval poet:

> He, of his gentleness,
> Thirsting and hungering
> Walked in the wilderness;
> Soft words of grace he spoke
> Unto lost desert-folk

> That listened wondering.
> He heard the bittern call
> From ruined palace-wall,
> Answered him brotherly;
> He held communion
> With the she-pelican
> Of lonely piety . . .

Other early poems—and later ones too—have the air of being sophisticated folk-poetry or even nursery rhymes, or work on the level of childhood or child-like myth, as in 'Warning to Children' and 'Lollocks'. The complex diversity of the physical world is reduced, in the first poem, to a kind of game, beyond which lie unspoken terrors:

> Children, if you dare to think
> Of the greatness, rareness, muchness,
> Fewness of this precious only
> Endless world in which you say
> You live, you think of things like this:
> Blocks of slate enclosing dappled
> Red and green, enclosing tawny
> Yellow nets, enclosing white
> And black acres of dominoes . . .

These almost toy-like properties endlessly repeat themselves, like a nightmarish parody of 'reality'—and what is at the bottom of it all? Whatever it is, Graves seems to suggest, we can never find it, even if we 'untie the string'. In the same way, the Lollocks are inexplicable, malevolent presences; all we can do is blame them for their daily horrors, and attempt to keep them at bay by being neat and orderly. Whether we are rational or irrational, they exist and we cannot ignore them:

> Sovereign against Lollocks
> Are hard broom and soft broom,
> To well comb the hair,
> To well brush the shoe,
> And to pay every debt
> So soon as it's due.

Such whimsical flirtations with horror are not cosily neutralized by being put in such terms; they employ that 'cool web of language' which (in his poem 'The Cool Web') is seen as a way of coping with experience:

> Children are dumb to say how hot the day is,
> How hot the scent is of the summer rose,
> How dreadful the black wastes of evening sky,
> How dreadful the tall soldiers drumming by.
>
> But we have speech, to chill the angry day,
> And speech, to dull the rose's cruel scent.
> We spell away the overhanging night,
> We spell away the soldiers and the fright . . .

This delicate, troubled poise is typical of Graves: stylish, subdued, deeply romantic in feeling but usually laconic in expression. His scrupulous, terse decorum is most apparent in his love poems, many of which exquisitely celebrate transience, chance, inevitability:

> Be warm, enjoy the season, lift your head,
> Exquisite in the pulse of tainted blood,
> That shivering glory not to be despised.
>
> Take your delight in momentariness,
> Walk between dark and dark, a shining space
> With the grave's narrowness, though not its peace.

Increasingly, Graves has come to see poetry as telling 'one story', of which there is only one theme and inspired by only one impulse—that of the Muse, the 'immanent Goddess'. Many of his poems during the past thirty years have been addresses to this figure, often an amalgam of an inspiring deity, a young woman adored by a much older man, and a character or characters (always female) out of distant but still passionate memory. The 'magic' element in all this, and Graves's abstruse, scholarly, but also eccentric and polemical delvings into mythology, history and religion, may have something in common (in their need for a framework, necessary to the poet if not to the reader) with Yeats's categorizing in *A Vision*; though Graves has made it clear

that he despises that side, and indeed most sides, of Yeats.
(Graves's Clark Lectures, incidentally, delivered at Cambridge in
1954–5, made hilariously unfair attacks on a whole range of
poets, from Pope and Wordsworth to Yeats, Pound, Eliot,
Auden and Dylan Thomas.) The difference lies partly in Graves's
reasonable and courtly unreason, his fastidiously classic tone as he
celebrates the irrational—in 'Dance of Words', for example:

> To make them move, you should start from lightning
> And not forecast the rhythm: rely on chance,
> Or so-called chance, for its bright emergence
> Once lightning interpenetrates the dance.
>
> Grant them their own traditional steps and postures
> But see they dance it out again and again
> Until only lightning is left to puzzle over—
> The choreography plain, and the theme plain.

Often he is arrogant, quizzical and sardonic, enjoying a talent
for light verse though he has affected to belittle Auden for such
things. In a short squib, he quotes (or pretends to quote—one
isn't always convinced about the accuracy of Graves's sources)
from a New York review:

Robert Graves, the British veteran, is no longer in the poetic swim.
He still resorts to traditional metres and rhyme, and to such outdated
words as *tilth*; witholding his 100% approbation also from contemporary poems that favour sexual freedom.

The poem 'Tilth' to which this is the epigraph runs:

> Gone are the drab monosyllabic days
> When 'agricultural labour' still was *tilth*;
> And '100% approbation', *praise*;
> And 'pornographic modernism', *filth*—
> Yet still I stand by *tilth* and *filth* and *praise*.

The wry sense of survival, mock embattled but perfectly sure of
itself, is part of the bitter-sweet taste of Graves's poetry, consistent with the man who revealed himself in *Goodbye to All That*
in 1929.

WILLIAM EMPSON

William Empson has published no new poems since his *Collected Poems* appeared in 1955, and the distinct stylistic influence he had on some poets in the 1950s (for which he has humorously disclaimed any responsibility) now looks like a minor by-way of literary history; but his best work (almost all of it written between 1929 and 1939) is still memorable and worth reading for its own sake. He was still an undergraduate when his poems attracted attention in Cambridge and beyond, being praised by (among others) the notoriously hard-to-please F. R. Leavis in *New Bearings in English Poetry*. While he was writing these early poems, he was also working on his pioneer book of literary analysis, *Seven Types of Ambiguity*, and the teasing, fine-drawn quality of his mind is evident in both. Indeed, Empson's ideas about poetic ambiguity are one of the pointers into his poetry. Part of this is his feeling for Donne and for the Metaphysical poets of the seventeenth century; as he jokingly put it many years later, when he began writing he 'thought it would be very nice to write beautiful things like the poet Donne. I would sit by the fire trying to think of an interesting puzzle.' This might be plain (though the poem is not) from such lines as

> Spears pierce its desert basin, the long dawn:
> Tower, noon, all cliquant, dock-side cranes, sag-fruited:
> And, sand-borne weight, brief by waste sand upborne,
> Leave, gulfed, ere night, the bare plain, deeper rooted.

One gets a hint as to how Empson wrote like this, and why he fails in such a passage as the stanza just quoted, in a note to another poem, where he says of an idea (an ambiguity, in fact) that he 'failed to get that into the line'; one has a mental picture of Empson assiduously loading every rift with ore. But these poems are not mere bits of fanciful juggling or strainingly subtle riddles. When they are impenetrable, one ought to ask whether this is not because so many of them seem to be concerned with incommunicability itself, with the isolation of human beings, as in the fine

'To an Old Lady'. Here he illustrates the poem's central figure by references to *King Lear*, the movement and substance of planets, the habits of bees and the fact that the universe is finite but unbounded; but he lets enough light show between the lines, despite their compact allusiveness, for the seriously tender feeling to come through:

> Ripeness is all; her in her cooling planet
> Revere; do not presume to think her wasted.
> Project her no projectile, plan nor man it;
> Gods cool in turn, by the sun long outlasted . . .
>
> Stars how much further from me fill my night.
> Strange that she too should be inaccessible,
> Who shares my sun. He curtains her from sight,
> And but in darkness is she visible.

A good deal has been made of Empson's early training as a mathematician; but the central point in his poetry, far more important than his eagerness to draw mathematical or scientific analogies or wring the last drop of juice out of an ambiguity, can be found in one of his notes (in the *Collected Poems*) to the poem 'Bacchus': 'Life involves maintaining oneself between contradictions that can't be solved by analysis'. This lies behind some of his best poems, both conversational ('Reflection from Rochester', 'Courage means Running') and highly-wrought ('Aubade', 'This Last Pain', 'Missing Dates'). In the second group, there is a strange tension between the delicate music of the adopted verse-schemes (*terza rima*, the villanelle, the aubade) and the often baleful passion of what is said, so that the repetitions and inversions become, in turn, menacing, wistful, savage, resigned. 'Aubade', for example, is a laconic meditation in a time of approaching war (*The Gathering Storm* was the title of Empson's second book of poems, published in 1940), poised between the repeated antitheses 'It seemed the best thing to be up and go' and 'The heart of standing is you cannot fly'. These refrains yoke together the themes of earthquake, adultery and war, so that the whole poem works on at least three levels. Beginning with the real earthquake (in Japan, where Empson was teaching in the 1930s), it moves on to his own insecurity, in a particular—though perhaps casual—guilty human relationship and in the world's chaos, for which the earthquake is itself an emblem; it cannot be escaped from, either by physical flight or in dreams:

> I slept, and blank as that I would yet lie.
> Till you have seen what a threat holds below,
> The heart of standing is you cannot fly.

Bodily escape, through movement or temporary physical gratification ('A bedshift flight to a Far Eastern sky'), bring one back, paradoxically, only to where one started from:

> But as to risings, I can tell you why.
> It is on contradiction that they grow.
> It seemed the best thing to be up and go.
> Up was the heartening and the strong reply,
> The heart of standing is we cannot fly.

'Up', therefore, to face those things from which 'we cannot fly': contradictions demand courage.

It is a moral honesty (or 'wise patience' as he applies it in 'Courage means Running') which is precarious rather than pedantic, stabilizing itself only momentarily with such pessimistic resonances as

> The waste remains, the waste remains and kills . . .
> I have mislaid the torment and the fear . . .
> Leave what you die for and be safe to die . . .

The conversational poems argue through contradictions or alternatives in a more relaxed way, with a wry humour which is closer to the surface, as in the conclusion to 'Ignorance of Death':

> Because we have neither hereditary nor direct knowledge of death
> It is the trigger of the literary man's biggest gun
> And we are happy to equate it to any conceived calm.
>
> Heaven me, when a man is ready to die about something
> Other than himself, and is in fact ready because of that,
> Not because of himself, that is something clear about himself.

> Otherwise I feel very blank upon this topic,
> And think that though important, and proper for anyone to bring
>
> up,
> It is one that most people should be prepared to be blank upon.

'Blank' and 'blankness', both in this sense of undogmatic open-
ness and in the sense of a terrified emptiness, are favourite words
of Empson's. The limitations of the rational intelligence, of wit
and sophistication—the limitations, in fact, of his own methods—
are themselves ironically questioned. The tensions and contradictions are recognized and, through Empson's agility, reconciled
—if only in the temporary peace that is a poem.

EDWIN MUIR

The forms and language which Edwin Muir used were always
traditional, and it is partly for this reason, no doubt, that he was
neglected for so long; in the words of Michael Roberts (who
thereby excluded his work from the original version of the *Faber
Book of Modern Verse* in 1936), he had not 'been compelled to
make any notable development of poetic technique'. Since then,
in the 1950s, he was given a measure of respect and reappraisal,
being seen by some as a father-figure, along with Graves and
Empson, of the poetic tone of that decade.

If one takes more than a summary glance at the *Collected Poems*,
one notices how freshly he worked within a traditional framework; even the archaisms have their place in the 'timelessness' of
his scheme. The movement is easy, the language transparent,
there are regularly organized stanzas, a general predominance of
rhyme, a liking for lyrical metres, and a certain amount of blank
verse; but the general effect is by no means second-hand. Read
together, the poems trace a painful spiritual journey which he
began long before he started to write poetry. In his classic *Autobiography*, Muir told with his habitual clarity and honesty of his
early upbringing: born on a remote island in the Orkneys, and

then plunged, while little more than a child, into a dreary life of menial jobs in Glasgow. When, much later, he discovered himself as a poet, he found great difficulty in expressing himself adequately:

> I had no training; I was too old to submit myself to contemporary influences; and I had acquired in Scotland a deference towards ideas which made my entry into poetry difficult. Though my imagination had begun to work, I had no technique by which I could give expression to it. There were the rhythms of English poetry on the one hand, the images in my mind on the other. All I could do at the start was to force the one, creaking and complaining, into the mould of the other . . . I began to write poetry simply because what I wanted to say could not have gone properly into prose. I wanted so much to say it that I had no thought left to study the form in which alone it could be said.

In the *Collected Poems*, Muir omitted a great deal of his early work; but among the few surviving examples of what he was writing in about 1925, there are poems such as 'Childhood', 'Horses' and 'Ballad of Hector in Hades' which are as good as anything he ever wrote, and which are stylistically very little different from several poems he wrote later. The Hector poem, drawing as it does on both traditional myth and personal experience, is typical. Muir wrote of the influence which his childhood had had on his poetry:

> These years . . . had come alive, after being forgotten for so long and when I wrote about horses they were my father's plough-horses as I saw them when I was four or five; and a poem on Achilles pursuing Hector round the walls of Troy was really resuscitation of the afternoon when I ran away, in real terror, from another boy as I returned from school.

This memory is authentically described, grafted naturally on to the Hector–Achilles story:

> The grasses puff a little dust
>   Where my footsteps fall.
> I cast a shadow as I pass
>   The little wayside wall.

> The strip of grass on either hand
>   Sparkles in the light;
> I only see that little space
>   To the left and to the right.
>
> And in that space our shadows run,
>   His shadow there and mine,
> The little flowers, the tiny mounds,
>   The grasses frail and fine.

The way in which this falls into simple ballad-like quatrains underlines a point made by T. S. Eliot after Muir's death, that he seemed not much concerned with technique 'but under the pressure of emotional intensity, and possessed by his vision, he found almost unconsciously the right, the inevitable way of saying what he wanted to say'.

Time is a central presence in his poems—a force which is a wheel rather than a river, turning again and again, and always moving through a predestined course; but without any of the elaborate perspectives Yeats imported into *A Vision*:

> There is a road that turning always
>   Cuts off the country of Again.
> Archers stand there on every side
>   And as it runs time's deer is slain,
>   And lies where it has lain . . .
>
> There the beginning finds the end
>   Before beginning ever can be,
> And the great runner never leaves
>   The starting and the finishing tree,
>   The budding and the fading tree.

His work is full of journeys, voyages, races and returns; indeed, he wrote at different times three separate poems called 'The Return'. Muir personifies such recurrence in different ways: sometimes the Greeks returning from Troy, sometimes Ulysses alone come back after his wandering, sometimes an old man looking back at his life and reliving it by remembering it, sometimes the poet himself returning to the Orkneys of his childhood. In his early and middle poems, Time is also the annihilator, the insuperable force which makes all our ideas of reality meaningless.

But in his middle fifties Muir became a Christian, and after that Time became the bond which links us with 'a Child, a God . . . a Birth, a Death'; man's birth and death are given significance because they mark the two poles of existence which Christ, too, experienced in his life on earth:

> Make me to see and hear that I may know
> The journey and the place towards which I go;
> For a beginning and an end are mine
> Surely, and have their sign
> Which I and all in the earth and the heavens show.
> Teach me to know.

But it is not a placid poetry of acceptance: anxieties and fears are often just below the surface, sometimes expressed in terms of symbolic archetypes (as in the struggle between the 'crested animal in his pride' and the 'soft round beast as brown as clay' in 'The Combat'), or with the strange clarity of a dream (as in 'The Horses' and 'I see the image of a naked man'), or in more contemporary terms, as in 'The Interrogation', which probably stems from his eyewitness view of Czechoslovakia in 1948:

> We cannot choose
> Answer or action here,
> Though still the careless lovers saunter by
> And the thoughtless field is near.
> We are on the very edge,
> Endurance almost done,
> And still the interrogation is going on.

Muir seemed totally—but not arrogantly—unconcerned with trends or fashions. He realized that he sometimes lacked 'freedom and inventiveness' in his poems, but, as he wrote in a letter:

> I think we are all far too much moved by a spirit of emulation, and when something 'new' appears feel almost in conscience bound to produce something new, whereas if we wrote from the solidest basis within ourselves we should produce something that is new.

CHAPTER ELEVEN

Philip Larkin (1922–)
Ted Hughes (1930–)

Philip Larkin published his first book of poems, *The North Ship*, in 1945, when he was in his early twenties. It was a precocious start, but an uncertain one; it would be difficult to guess that here were the beginnings of a considerable poet, and indeed it attracted little attention. The poems are careful, yearning, touched here and there with signs of devotion to Yeats (though not the later Yeats) and to Auden. But it was in the year following the publication of *The North Ship* that Larkin wrote the first poems of his maturity: 'Waiting for breakfast' (which is attached as a 'coda' to the 1966 reissue of *The North Ship*) and 'Wedding-wind', chronologically the first piece in *The Less Deceived*, his second book, published in 1955. One of the things they do is to mark the liberation and sense of direction which reading Hardy's poems gave Larkin; for, though they show no overt influence of Hardy, they reflect something of the 'human shows' of Hardy's work, a congenial way of using personal experience without attaching oneself to (as Larkin has put it) 'a concept of poetry that lay outside my own life . . . One could simply relapse back into one's own life and write from it'.

This does not mean that Larkin's poems are wholly personal in the sense of being 'I'-centred. In fact the voice of 'Wedding-wind' is in no useful sense that of the poet. A woman on the morning after her wedding night is wonderingly turning over the fact of her happiness, with the force of the high wind 'bodying-forth' not only the irrelevance of such violent elements to the new delight she has found, but also the way in which the whole of creation seems somehow to be in union with her state:

> Can it be borne, this bodying-forth by wind
> Of joy my actions turn on, like a thread
> Carrying beads? Shall I be let to sleep
> Now this perpetual morning shares my bed?
> Can even death dry up
> These new delighted lakes, conclude
> Our kneeling as cattle by all-generous waters?

Yet though it is happy and joyous, it is not quite serene: it implies, in its three closing questions, the impermanence of the very happiness it celebrates, the possibility of its being blown and scattered, made restless as the horses have been and

> All's ravelled under the sun by the wind blowing.

This emotional wariness is typical of Larkin, though 'Wedding-wind' is not a typical Larkin poem. It has been said that he is 'the poet of the void. The one affirmation his work offers is the possibility that when we have lost everything the problem of beauty will still remain.' Though there is a sense in which this is a very perceptive observation, it is perhaps truer to what one feels about the later books (*The Whitsun Weddings* and *High Windows*) than it is to *The Less Deceived*. On the other hand, it is peculiarly difficult (and may be a waste of time) to read through the three books of Larkin's maturity in search of 'development'. From *The Less Deceived* on, the personality is an achieved and consistent one, each poem restating or adding another facet to what has gone before.

Though there has been no radical development in Larkin's poetry since he found his own voice, the number of tones he has used has been very varied. The 'emotional wariness' can in some of the poems be better defined as an agnostic stoicism in face of the passing of time and 'the only end of age': death. There are poems in which time, and death as the yardstick of time, are seen in an abstract or generalized context: 'Ignorance', 'Triple Time', 'Next Please', 'Nothing to be Said', 'Going', 'Wants', 'Age'. They are abstract or generalized in that they do not start from some posited situation, though their language and imagery are certainly concrete: the street, sky and landscape of 'Triple Time', for example, or the 'armada of promises' of 'Next Please'. In this second poem, the simple notion at the beginning is that, like Mr Micawber, we are always waiting for something to 'turn up'. Larkin uses as his image of these elusive hopes the proverbial ship (as in the phrase 'When my ship comes in'); the difference is that this 'armada of promises' is concretely drawn, a literal fleet, appearing, and then disappearing, on the horizon. But none of these is 'our ship', only the ship of destiny or fate which follows behind us, carrying oblivion with it. Notice the contrast—typical of Larkin—between the easy, conversational first stanza:

> Always too eager for the future, we
> Pick up bad habits of expectancy.
> Something is always approaching; every day
> *Till then* we say . . .

and the superbly controlled foreboding of the last stanza:

> Only one ship is seeking us, a black-
> Sailed unfamiliar, towing at her back
> A huge and birdless silence. In her wake
> No waters breed or break.

In a statement he made in 1955, Larkin said:

I write poems to preserve things I have seen/thought/felt (if I may so indicate a composite and complex experience) both for myself and for others, though I feel that my prime responsibility is to the experience itself, which I am trying to keep from oblivion for its own sake. Why I should do this I have no idea, but I think the impulse to preserve lies at the bottom of all art.

And a later comment:

Some years ago I came to the conclusion that to write a poem was to construct a verbal device that would preserve an experience indefinitely by reproducing it in whoever read the poem.

This 'verbal pickling' (as he put it) is seen to be the process at work in many of his best and best-known poems: 'Church Going', 'The Whitsun Weddings', 'Mr Bleaney', 'Reference Back', 'I

Remember, I Remember', 'Dockery and Son', 'Sad Steps', 'Show Saturday'. All of these start from some specifically recalled incident which becomes, through the course of the poem, 'an experience' in the sense intended by Larkin in that prose note. Each both preserves the experience and allows it to move out into other areas not predicted by the casually 'placing' opening lines. Indeed, in several of them the placing, the observation, is steadily sustained for a considerable part of the poem, as if the 'impulse to preserve' were determined to fix and set the moment with every aspect carefully delineated, every shade faithfully recorded.

'Church Going' moves, through seven carefully-patterned nine-line stanzas, from easy, colloquial, mockingly casual beginnings, through reflection and half-serious questioning, to a rhetorical solidity at the close—a conclusion that is not an attempt to endorse Christianity but an acknowledgement of the strange power of inherited order and habit:

> A serious house on serious earth it is,
> In whose blent air all our compulsions meet,
> Are recognized, and robed as destinies.
> And that much never can be obsolete,
> Since someone will forever be surprising
> A hunger in himself to be more serious,
> And gravitating with it to this ground,
> Which, he once heard, was proper to grow wise in,
> If only that so many dead lie round.

In 'The Whitsun Weddings', the level descriptive sweep, the amused human observation, move with complete inevitability to the mysterious closing lines as the train with its load of newly-married couples slows as it reaches its destination:

> And as the tightened brakes took hold, there swelled
> A sense of falling, like an arrow-shower
> Sent out of sight, somewhere becoming rain.

The force of this is partly cumulative (and notice how each ten-line stanza seems caught on the pivot of the short four-syllable second line, pushing it forward on to the next smooth run), but it has a lot to do with Larkin's unerring ear for individual cadences—that 'sense of falling' one hears in

> So
> To pile them back, to cry,
> Was hard, without lamely admitting how
> It had not done so then, and could not now.
> ('Love Songs in Age')

> They show us what we have as it once was,
> Blindingly undiminished, just as though
> By acting differently we could have kept it so.
> ('Reference Back')

> Life is first boredom, then fear.
> Whether or not we use it, it goes,
> And leaves what something hidden from us chose,
> And age, and then the only end of age.
> ('Dockery and Son')

Sometimes Larkin deals with his habitual themes of diminution, decay, death, in an extreme and even savage way, as he does in 'Sunny Prestatyn', in which the blandishments of the girl on the poster have been desecrated and disproved. The opening of 'The Old Fools' has something of the same feeling:

> What do they think has happened, the old fools,
> To make them like this? Do they somehow suppose
> It's more grown-up when your mouth hangs open and drools,
> And you keep on pissing yourself and can't remember
> Who called this morning?

But such savagery always turns back on itself in Larkin, often seen with fear and horror. Detail, and a treatment of that detail with what Larkin (talking about John Betjeman's poems) has called 'an almost moral tactfulness', is one way of steadying the gaze in the face of such things—as in 'The Building', perhaps Larkin's finest poem. It opens with a typically dense and carefully selected proliferation of impressionist detail, so organized that it is only gradually one realizes that the place being described is a hospital. As in 'Church Going' and 'The Whitsun Weddings', the detail is an embodiment of the poem, not the casual decoration its colloquial ease may first suggest:

> on the way
> Someone's wheeled past, in washed-to-rags ward clothes:
> They see him, too. They're quiet. To realize
> This new thing held in common makes them quiet,
> For past these doors are rooms, and rooms past those,
> And more rooms yet, each one further off
> And harder to return from . . .

And in the end, relentlessly poised like the train in 'The Whitsun Weddings', the realization towards which the whole delicate structure has been aimed is achieved:

> All know they are going to die.
> Not yet, perhaps not here, but in the end,
> And somewhere like this. That is what it means,
> This clean-sliced cliff; a struggle to transcend
> The thought of dying, for unless its powers
> Outbuild cathedrals nothing contravenes
> The coming dark, though crowds each evening try
>
> With wasteful, weak, propitiatory flowers.

Even Larkin's least elevated, most casually light poems have a refined, unobtrusive, but technically formidable skill, able to accommodate colloquial language and colloquial rhythms, as in 'Toads', 'Toads Revisited', 'Naturally the Foundation Will Bear Your Expenses', 'Posterity', and 'Vers de Société', which balances boring sociability against the pleasures and desolations of solitude. Both serious and light have the distinctive, subtle, often rueful if not sad, flavour of an individual, with the loyalties, exasperations, illuminations and speaking voice of a 'character'. Part of Larkin's breadth of appeal comes from the many kinds of poem in which this character can appear; from the evocation of nineteenth-century emigrants (in 'How Distant') or colliers (in 'The Explosion') to the lyrical naturalism of 'The Trees' and 'Cut Grass', the breadth of sympathies is wide, however wan the tone. He is a memorable poet without being an easy one from whom to quote in single lines and phrases, for his effects are total; but even so there are such extraordinary lines as

> Such attics cleared of me! Such absences!

and

> Or spoor of pads, or a bird's adept splay

and

> An air lambent with adult enterprise

and

> The glare of that much-mentioned brilliance, love

and (self-mockingly)

> O wolves of memory! Immensements!

Individual though Larkin is, he often reflects common experiences and common concerns. He has no easy answers, but he does not wallow in fashionable *angst* either. As far as 'public' concerns go, he has touched on such things in some poems (such as 'Going, Going' and 'Homage to a Government'), showing attitudes that are conservative and even 'reactionary'—in this, though in little else, reminding one of Yeats and Eliot. But unlike any other important modern British poet (with the exception of the otherwise utterly different Dylan Thomas), Larkin has constructed no system into which his poems can fit: like Parolles in Shakespeare's *All's Well*, he seems to say 'simply the thing I am shall make me live'.

TED HUGHES

The most massive and influential force in English poetry in the 1960s and since is often taken to be Ted Hughes. Within a decade of the publication of his first book, *The Hawk in the Rain* (1957), he was accepted as a classic of our time, some of his books becoming set texts in schools—the most practical form of approval that a living poet can expect. Very large critical claims have been made for Hughes: A. Alvarez, for example, has called him 'a poet of the first importance'.

The poems in the first two books, *The Hawk in the Rain* and then *Lupercal* (1960), mainly concentrated on physical vividness of a kind that was certainly unignorable. The Hughes world was one that was turbulently full of predatory animals, primitive violence, and moments of extreme human endurance—a bloody world ruled by impulse and instinct, in which there were

> No indolent procrastinations and no yawning stares,
> No sighs or head-scratchings. Nothing but bounce and stab
> And a ravening second.

There is a profusion of creatures in Hughes's work, almost a modern bestiary: hawks, jaguars, a macaw, foxes, horses, wolves, pike, gnats, flies, monkeys, skylarks, rats, bears, spiders, crabs, pigs, bulls, otters, crows—and these not just as decorative images or grace-notes but as the central emblems. Hughes was brought up in parts of the Yorkshire Pennines which in the 1930s and 1940s still formed a kind of strange hinterland between the old, wild, rural West Riding and the collieries—a landscape that shared something in its character with the Nottinghamshire–Derbyshire border where D. H. Lawrence spent his childhood; and it is not only in his forceful exactness about rural things that Hughes sometimes reminds one of Lawrence.

'His images have an admirable violence', wrote Edwin Muir in a review of *The Hawk in the Rain*, and the violence is that of Tennyson's line from *In Memoriam*: 'Nature red in tooth and claw.' Human life, too, is seen in terms of brute physical activity, and in the first two books there is a particular obsession with the animal-like trench-fighting of the First World War, in which Hughes's father and uncles fought. Many of the poems can be seen as parables of human life, but generally expressed in such spurts of energy that the tamed and untamed worlds blur. A well-known example of this is one of Hughes's most anthologized poems, 'The Thought-Fox': it gives a good picture of the physical origin, and physical impact, of his work. The fox becomes the poem, the poem becomes the fox, a presence gradually approaching,

> Brilliantly, concentratedly,
> Coming about its own business
>
> Till, with a sudden sharp hot stink of fox
> It enters the dark hole of the head.
> The window is starless still; the clock ticks,
> The page is printed.

In the earlier poems the physical energy sometimes turns blustering and incoherent; there is some verbal grotesqueness (e.g. 'how loud and above what / Furious spaces of fire do the distracting devils / Orgy and hosannah . . .') and turbulent diction ('The cradled guns, damascus, blued, flared'). But elsewhere he manages something altogether sparer, equally 'tough' but without clogged over-writing. 'Hawk Roosting' and 'View of a Pig' are good examples. The first, a monologue of the hawk itself, has a plain sense of unadorned address, very suitable for the arrogant simplicity of the speaker:

> The convenience of the high trees!
> The air's buoyancy and the sun's ray
> Are of advantage to me;
> And the earth's face upward for my inspection.
>
> My feet are locked upon the rough bark.
> It took the whole of creation
> To produce my foot, my each feather:
> Now I hold creation in my foot
>
> Or fly up, and revolve it all slowly . . .
>
> The sun is behind me.
> Nothing has changed since I began.
> My eye has permitted no change.
> I am going to keep things like this.

There is also much of the sea, as the first fierce chaos and the destructive eater of the land. In 'Pibroch' (from Hughes's book

Wodwo, 1967) the sea, a stone, the wind, a tree, are all seen as caught up in a vortex of change and destruction:

> Minute after minute, aeon after aeon,
> Nothing lets up or develops.
> And this is neither a bad variant nor a tryout.
> This is where the staring angels go through.
> This is where all the stars bow down.

This war between annihilation and survival, between Genesis and Armageddon, has increasingly been expressed in forms influenced by primitive, oral poetry from the pre-literate world—Red Indian, Eskimo—which can sound like spells and mystic incantations. Such features are particularly apparent in *Crow*, which Hughes published in 1970. This sequence, which was described by the poet on its first appearance as 'the passages of verse from about the first two-thirds of what was to have been an epic folktale', has been controversial from the beginning. To some it is a major poem, a work of genius; the central character, Crow himself, has been described as 'a new hero'—though that may have been ironically meant. Others have written of Hughes's 'apparently deliberate resort to primitive ham-fisted adjectives and trudging monosyllabic phrases', and his 'mechanical, drugging repetition'. Whatever the consensus, *Crow* has certainly entered the poetry-reading consciousness, and its manner or manners have been widely imitated and even parodied—a firm indication that a work has 'arrived'.

Crow basically has two characters—Crow and God. Crow is resilient, resourceful, evasive, built to survive every kind of disaster. God is sometimes his partner, sometimes his adversary or rival, often a passive presence who goes on sleeping while Crow gets up to his gruesome tricks:

> Crow laughed.
> He bit the Worm, God's only son,
> Into two writhing halves.
>
> He stuffed into man the tail half
> With the wounded end hanging out.

> He stuffed the head half headfirst into woman
> And it crept in deeper and up
> To peer out through her eyes
> Calling its tail-half to join up quickly, quickly
> Because O it was painful.

The manner of *Crow* is almost all like this—a series of unmodified narrative accounts of brutally comic (or just brutally brutal) events, sometimes varied with catalogues of incantations or lists of questions—common devices in the oral poetry I have mentioned. There are a few key words—black, blood, smashed, stabbed, screamed. It is hard to avoid the impression that one is being offered a portentous and heavily loaded creation-and-destruction myth in a single package.

Since the publication of *Crow*, Ted Hughes seems to have followed two paths, which still continue. One is in the direction of an even more severe fragmentation, in the sequences called 'Prometheus on his Rock' and 'Lumb's Remains'; the other, though presented as poetry for children, has all the forceful keensightedness of his earlier work and makes no compromises, though there is a firmer grip on form; and poems of this kind can be found in his book *Season Songs* (1976).

CHAPTER TWELVE

Poetry Since 1965

Although I have said that Ted Hughes has been 'a massive and influential force' in English poetry since the 1960s, one of the things to notice about the post-war scene is how various and heterogeneous it has been. In the 1950s Graves, Muir and Empson, different from one another as they were, became admired (and in some cases imitated) as they had not been before. The so-called 'Movement' was seen as taking them as exemplars and father-figures. This 'Movement' was in fact given its blankly anonymous title by an article which appeared in the *Spectator* in October 1954; the writer (also anonymous) spoke of 'the emergence of a new movement', hostile to the 1930s and 1940s, influenced by Leavis, Empson, Orwell and Graves, 'not much interested in suffering, and extremely impatient of poetic sensibility', 'anti-phoney ... anti-wet; sceptical, robust, ironic'. Within the next two years two anthologies appeared, D. J. Enright's *Poets of the 1950s* in Japan (where Enright was teaching at the time) and Robert Conquest's *New Lines* in Britain. Both drew on the same contributors, and these were those who had been named or hinted at in the *Spectator* article. Neither Enright nor Conquest made any firm show of launching, or even of recognizing, any such thing as a Movement ('It will be seen at once', wrote Conquest in his introduction to *New Lines*, 'that these poets do not have as much in common as they would if they were a group of doctrine-saddled writers forming a definite school complete with programme and rules'). Nevertheless, the nine poets in these anthologies—Conquest and Enright themselves, Kingsley Amis, Donald Davie, Thom Gunn, John Holloway, Philip Larkin, John Wain and Elizabeth Jennings—were as firmly docketed with a common label as any doctrine could possibly have achieved.

Since then, most of these poets have more clearly gone their different ways. Philip Larkin was early on recognized as the most outstanding of them. Elizabeth Jennings and D. J. Enright, who even in 1956 seemed uneasy inhabitants of *New Lines*, have confirmed their differences in later work. Elizabeth Jennings's *Collected Poems*, published in 1967, gathered what she had written over a period of fifteen years and showed a steady and persistent contemplative gift, rational but open to mystery, tender but on the whole unsentimental, expressed in forms and words that were almost always pure, clear, gravely lyrical and committed to a sense of hard-won order out of chaos. Enright has gone on with his humane, amusing, commonsensical, wanly indignant notations of the social brutalities and masqueradings of a world he knows well—from Thailand to the English Midlands, from Japan to Germany—in a loose-limbed style that is sometimes biting, sometimes slapdash.

The three *New Lines* poets who have gone furthest in changing what had been their early manners are John Wain, Donald Davie and Thom Gunn. Each has followed a different progression— Wain from metronomic verse much influenced by Empson (Wain's essay on Empson, 'Ambiguous Gifts', published in the last number of *Penguin New Writing* in 1950, was instrumental in drawing attention to a poet neglected at that time) to free-ranging and sometimes garrulous poems; Davie from polished epigrammatic lines (in a poem written in the 1950s he referred to himself sardonically as 'A pasticheur of late-Augustan styles') to much more open and ambitious work; and Gunn from what he has called his early 'clenched' verse—tough, cynical, hard-edged, as in 'On the Move'—through freer and more tentative poems, influenced by some contemporary American poets such as Gary Snyder, to the sensuous but again tense and disciplined work in *Moly* (1971) and *Jack Straw's Castle* (1976).

In the aftermath of the Movement, another loose assemblage of poets was noticed: this was 'The Group', a discussion-group or workshop of poets who met week by week in the later 1950s and through the 1960s. Whatever unity it may have had (and when *A Group Anthology* was published in 1963, some reviewers, mostly hostile, fancied there *was* some sort of unity), there is more point now in looking at the individual achievements of a handful of Group attenders who, like the 'members' of the Movement, have confirmed their differences rather than their similarities. The positive effect of the Group was probably that it gave people the opportunity for strenuous critical searching and self-searching in an atmosphere in which (as Edward Lucie-Smith, in whose house the Group met for most of its years, put it) all accepted that 'poetry is discussable . . . that the process by which words work in poetry is something open to rational examination'.

Peter Porter is in many ways the most successful of these former Group participants. In his first book (*Once Bitten Twice Bitten*, 1961) he seemed primarily a satirist, a fierce but also witty demolisher of social aspirations, the rich, the smug, the phoney, 'the smoothies of our Elizabethan age'. But gradually he has emerged more solidly (and no less entertainingly) as an elegiac poet; Porter himself has said that from the beginning his poems 'have polarized about the art and life of the past and the everyday world of the present', so that in his work the Holy Roman Empire, the experimental composer John Cage, Bach, advertising slogans, Carthage, Beverly Hills and the Black Country all co-exist as living parts of the continuous world of the imagination. Some of his most skilful work in this mingled area of past and present has been in his versions of Martial, the Roman poet of the first century AD. Porter has remodelled many of Martial's epigrams, freely using anachronism as a telescoping device in the cause of vividness and relevance. His most anthologized piece, 'Your Attention Please', is a grimly flat, mordantly colloquial radio announcement of an imminent nuclear strike, and reflects very well a mood of the late 1950s and early 1960s; but he can be much more rich and dense, as in such poems as 'Seahorses', 'Fossil Gathering' and 'An Angel in Blythburgh Church'.

Other Group members who have written varied and interesting poems are Alan Brownjohn, Edwin Brock, George MacBeth and Peter Redgrove. Alan Brownjohn's distinctiveness (and one could say the same of Porter's 'Your Attention Please') cannot be guessed from his best-known piece, the poem which begins 'We are going to see the rabbit', a childlike exercise in the manner of Jacques Prévert. Brownjohn himself has said that a number of his poems tend towards 'the condition of fiction', almost as situations or incidents from a novel or short story: characters are revealed obliquely or through their own monologues—a girl disc-jockey, a smart young executive, salesmen and antique dealers and politicians. It is as if cross-sections of human relationships and social or work situations are offered for our wry appraisal. Brock is more straightforward, making neatly devastating points about violence and heartlessness in 'Five Ways to Kill a Man' and 'Song of the Battery Hen', and laconically humorous self-observations:

> These are my credentials:
> I am clever
> and I am aware.
>
> You buy me
> in a small transparent ball
> almost entirely filled with water.
> You shake me
> and a plastic snowstorm
> will ensue.

George MacBeth is often a teasing and provocative writer, with a strong sense of play and performance (something I shall go into in more general terms about recent poetry a little later); but many of his best poems are autobiographical meditations which avoid spectacular tricks. Examples are 'The Miner's Helmet', 'The Drawer' and 'On the Death of May Street', in which the gruesome or ribald joker is totally absent. Finally, Peter Redgrove is a strenuously energetic and even extravagant poet, fuelled equally with violent (but also accurate) notions of science and with delvings into the occult—witchcraft, pantheism, cabbalistic and runic stuff. Some of his best work has been in the form of prose-poem monologues, such as 'Mr Waterman' and 'The Sermon', in which his taste for the grotesque is shown to advantage.

Many poets have, of course, stood quite apart from either the Movement or the Group. A poet who is a good deal older than any mentioned so far in this chapter, who has been publishing since the 1940s, but who came to proper recognition in the late 1950s, is R. S. Thomas. Thomas has spent most of his life working as a clergyman in the bleak depopulated hill country of mid-Wales, and it is the landscape of his poems, in which one senses several degrees of isolation. The land itself is remote from the big cities, unprofitable, a place where a man either tenuously survives or goes under. It has a past

> Brittle with relics,
> Wind-bitten towers and castles
> With sham ghosts;
> Mouldering quarries and mines

but it has nothing to do with the present, except as an impotent reminder of past glories. And the poet himself, though Welsh, is an outsider, living among the poor hill-farmers yet isolated because he is a priest and a poet, always observing from a distance. But his detachment is unjudging, and he feels strongly for this dying race,

> Castaways on a sea
> Of grass, who call to me,
> Clinging to their doomed farms;
> Their hearts though rough are warm
> And firm, and their slow wake
> Through time bleeds for our sake.

What emerges is a sense of the obdurate nature of life, a belief in resilience and dogged survival. The beliefs are pessimistic, and there is often a suggestion of bitterness: in 'The Welsh Hill Country', the person addressed—the reader—is taken to be someone who is looking for conventional rural delights:

> The sheep are grazing at Bwlch-y-Fedwen,
> Arranged romantically in the usual manner
> On a bleak background of bald stone,

and who therefore misses the realities of decay, disease, deprivation. It is all 'Too far for you to see'. The words 'bleak' and 'bald' are frequent in Thomas, augmented with 'gaunt', 'stark', 'dark', 'rain' and 'cold'. With these, one can contrast his almost obsessive mention of 'blood' as the single brightly coloured element in an otherwise monotone landscape; sometimes the actual blood that comes from real wounds, as in 'January':

> The fox drags its wounded belly
> Over the snow, the crimson seeds
> Of blood burst with a mild explosion,
> Soft as excrement, bold as roses.

The movement of his poems is mostly a severely checked free verse, which has increasingly become more severe and uncompromising, as in 'H'm', the title-poem of one of his recent books, and itself a baleful brief shudder. Thomas's special achievement is to have given intense and memorable substance to a narrow, almost Calvinist view of the world, by creating his own bleakly selective country, in which hills, valleys, stones, men and animals spell out lessons of courage in a hostile scheme of things.

A much younger poet who has been an equally isolated figure (though not in any geographical sense) is Geoffrey Hill. His dense, formal, formidable poems have gradually established themselves since the publication of *For the Unfallen* in 1959, and his two later books (*King Log*, 1968, and *Mercian Hymns*, 1971) have extended his readers. Hill's deeply serious concerns and the ceremonial exactness of his language were already apparent in poems written before he was twenty—in 'Genesis', 'Holy Thursday' and 'God's Little Mountain':

> Below, the river scrambled like a goat
> Dislodging stones. The mountain stamped its foot,
> Shaking, as from a trance. And I was shut
> With wads of sound into a sudden quiet.

These early poems, collected in *For the Unfallen*, have an ample but grimly controlled rhetoric which he continued to master. There is a rapt sense of struggle for exactness, for the precise word which will also be the resonant word, as in 'Where fish at dawn ignite the powdery lake', and a taut compression which sometimes becomes congestion, a tight-lipped ritualistic speech: the eight lines of 'Ovid in the Third Reich', for example, can lend

themselves to as much exegesis as there are hours in the day—
which is not to say that the effort is not worth it. The two substantial sequences in *King Log*—'Funeral Music' and 'The Songbook of Sebastian Arrurruz'—show distinct contrasts both in
theme and in the way Hill uses his compressed and chiselled
language. 'Funeral Music' consists of eight fourteen-line poems
suggested by bloody incidents during the fifteenth-century Wars
of the Roses: an attempt at what Hill has called 'a florid grim
music broken by grunts and shrieks'; in it, as elsewhere in Hill,
casual phrases and dead metaphors are 'rinsed and restored':

> A field
> After battle utters its own sound
> Which is like nothing on earth, but is earth.

The 'grim music' of the sequence is orchestrated in this fashion,
and the effect is both massive and finely sensitive. 'The Songbook
of Sebastian Arrurruz' purports to be the work of 'an apocryphal
Spanish poet'—a device which distances but does not coldly
objectify moods of regret and sexual desolation. Bitterness, loss,
hopeless sensuality conflict:

> There would have been things to say, quietness
> That could feed on our lust, refreshed
> Trivia, the occurrences of the day;
> And at night my tongue in your furrow.
>
> Without you I am mocked by courtesies
> And chat, where satisfied women push
> Dutifully towards some unneeded guest
> Desirable features of conversation.

The thirty prose poems that make up *Mercian Hymns* centre on
the eighth-century King of the West Midlands, Offa, but the
effort here is not towards the re-creation of the past as it was with
'Funeral Music'. The commanding and unifying figure is sometimes the ancient king, sometimes the poet himself in childhood
or present manhood: throughout the sequence, the remote past,
the recent past and the present are obliquely presented, often

within the space of a single section—as is plain from the beginning:

> King of the perennial holly-groves, the riven sandstone: overlord
> of the M5: architect of the historic rampart and ditch, the citadel at
> Tamworth, the summer hermitage in Holy Cross: guardian of
> the Welsh Bridge and the Iron Bridge: contractor to the desirable
> new estates: saltmaster: moneychanger: commissioner for oaths:
> martyrologist: the friend of Charlemagne.

> 'I liked that', said Offa, 'sing it again.'

The method and tone of *Mercian Hymns* (though they may owe
something to David Jones's *In Parenthesis* and *The Anathemata*)
are like nothing else in English: complex, rich, many-layered, an
intricately worked meditation on history, power, tradition, order
and memory, in which the precision of the language and the
mysterious reverberations of the past combine to achieve something completely inevitable and true.

Another poet who has more recently used the past as a way of
looking at the present is the Ulster writer, Seamus Heaney. He
began, in *Death of a Naturalist* (1966), as someone who had been
affected—though not in a slavish way—by Ted Hughes's 'nature'
poetry. Almost the whole of this first book drew on his own
childhood in rural Derry, and what was noticed immediately was
his verbal and physical sensuousness, fresh eyes and fresh phrases:

> As a child, they could not keep me from wells
> And old pumps with buckets and windlasses.
> I loved the dark drop, the trapped sky, the smells
> Of waterweed, fungus and dank moss.

Without losing this sensuousness, he has gradually shown an extension of range beyond country memories, and a progressive
tightening-up, an economical reduction to essentials. In 'Orange
Drums, Tyrone, 1966' he looks at a Protestant bandsman:

> To every cocked ear, expert in its greed,
> His battered signature subscribes 'No Pope'.
> The pigskin's scourged until his knuckles bleed.
> The air is pounding like a stethoscope.

But, digging further back—and a kind of delicate linguistic excavation is the method of much of Heaney's more recent poetry —he has found tangled continuities in the whole matter of Ireland:

> I push back
> through dictions,
> Elizabethan canopies,
> Norman devices,
>
> the erotic mayflowers
> of Provence
> and the ivied latins
> of churchmen
>
> to the scop's
> twang, the iron
> flash of consonants
> cleaving the line.

The invasions of the Scandinavians and the English, the subjugation of a people and their language, are explored in no political or sectarian way but with a strong sense of an ancient landscape. Comparisons have been made between Yeats and Seamus Heaney, but little more illuminatingly than to maintain that Heaney is the best Irish poet since Yeats: probably true, but their experiences and concerns are very different.

One obvious development in British poetry since about 1965 has been the emergence of so-called 'pop' poetry—not the only label, but a common and convenient one. It shared something with the rise of the Beatles in the early 1960s, and something too with the general atmosphere of dissent and protest that became vocal among many students in Britain between, say, the Suez invasion of 1956 and the end of the Vietnam war. The mass poetry-reading at the Albert Hall in London in June 1965 can be seen as the first concerted breakthrough, when 7,000 people unexpectedly turned up to hear, among others, Allen Ginsberg and Adrian Mitchell read poems. Mitchell's 'Tell me lies about Vietnam', read on that occasion, might be considered a showpiece of this kind of poetry. Mitchell shares with Christopher Logue a populist political sense, and at the same time a willingness to entertain an audience with what one might call moments of instant communion. At this level of simple directives—'laugh', 'cry', 'shout'—they are on the same platform as the poets who began to become known from Liverpool and Newcastle: Adrian Henri, Brian Patten, Roger McGough, Tom Pickard, Barry MacSweeney. But Mitchell and Logue have been more formidable, more serious, and in the past (though not for some years) have written well: Mitchell in 'The Fox', 'The Dust', 'Briefing', Logue in some of his ballads and earlier songs, 'The Story about the Road', and his version of part of the *Iliad*, 'Patrocleia'. Henri and the rest are, variously, clowns, entertainers, mild satirists, with various degrees of public skill. With all of them, including Mitchell and Logue, live performance is the essence of what they do, aiming for what Michael Horovitz (whose anthology, *Children of Albion*, published in 1969, is a sourcebook for most of those I have mentioned) has called 'a sacramental jubilee'. All these activities seemed to reach their peak of success and popularity in the late 1960s and early 1970s, but at the time of writing they are much less sympathetically listened to by young audiences than they were. In an odd way these poets, too, are now seen as belonging to an 'establishment', having been taught in schools and enthused about by teachers with supposedly progressive notions.

But one positive credit one should hand to this 'pop' movement is that it did help to create an audience, which for a time seemed unusually large, prepared to listen to poetry as an activity as normal and enjoyable as listening to music. Since about the mid-1960s very many poets have benefited from this, and not only ones of a 'pop' persuasion. There has been official recognition, through such efforts as the combined Arts Council–Department of Education & Science 'Writers in Schools' scheme, the National Poetry Secretariat (which acts as agent for organizations wanting poetry-readings by poets), and the schemes run by regional arts councils. Some poets (such as Philip Larkin) adamantly hold back from such things, but in general the move seems to have been a good one, and particularly in schools and colleges.

One could, at this point, collapse from heterogeneousness into chaos, if an attempt were made to go on itemizing current activity among poets in Britain. The followers of concrete poetry, sound poetry, found poetry; the clamorous activity in Wales and Scotland, quite apart from what seems to be a genuine renaissance of poetry in Ulster (for Seamus Heaney is not alone; there are at least half a dozen other Northern Irish poets at work today who are worth reading); the proliferation of 'little' magazines of every persuasion, some of them—such as the *New Review*—highly professional and heavily subsidized; and a considerable number of poets whom I am acutely conscious of having not even named, and whose work deserves to be read. As a short survey which has tried to be an introduction, this book has not aimed either to be all-inclusive or, at this point, prophetic. Living and working as I do, in the middle of the situation, it is difficult, if not impossible, to stand back and see any clear pattern in British poetry in the late 1970s. What is undeniable is that there is a great deal of it. As Yeats said on a famous occasion at the Cheshire Cheese (the London pub which was such a literary focus in the 1880s and 1890s), on a night when more poets than usual had come: 'None of us can say who will succeed, or even who has or who has not talent. The only thing certain about us is that we are too many.'

Select Bibliography

INDIVIDUAL POETS

Chapter 2

GERARD MANLEY HOPKINS: *Poems*, Oxford, 1948.
Selected Poems and Prose, Penguin, 1953.
W. H. GARDNER: *Gerard Manley Hopkins*, Secker & Warburg, 1948.
GEOFFREY GRIGSON: *Gerard Manley Hopkins*, Longman ('Writers & their Work'), 1955.

Chapter 3

W. B. YEATS: *Collected Poems*, Macmillan, 1950.
Autobiographies, Macmillan, 1955.
Mythologies, Macmillan, 1959.
Essays and Introductions, Macmillan, 1961.
Explorations, Macmillan, 1962.
A Vision, Macmillan, 1962.
Collected Plays, Macmillan, 1952.
Letters, Macmillan, 1954.
RICHARD ELLMANN: *Yeats: The Man and the Masks*, Macmillan, 1949.
The Identity of Yeats, Macmillan, 1954.
T. R. HENN: *The Lonely Tower*, Methuen, 1950.
J. M. HONE: *W. B. Yeats, 1865–1939*, Macmillan, 1962.
JON STALLWORTHY: *Between the Lines: Yeats's Poetry in the Making*, Oxford, 1963.
FRANK TUOHY: *W. B. Yeats*, Macmillan, 1976.

Chapter 4

WILFRED OWEN: *Collected Poems*, Chatto & Windus, 1963.
JON STALLWORTHY: *Wilfred Owen: a Biography*, Chatto, and Oxford, 1974.
D. S. R. WELLAND: *Wilfred Owen: a Critical Study*, Chatto & Windus, 1960.
EDWARD THOMAS: *Collected Poems*, Faber, 1936.
WILLIAM COOKE: *Edward Thomas: a Critical Biography*, Faber, 1970.
ELEANOR FARJEON: *Edward Thomas: the Last Four Years*, Oxford University Press, 1958.

VERNON SCANNELL: *Edward Thomas*, Longman ('Writers & their Work'), 1963.

HELEN THOMAS: *As It Was and World Without End*, Faber, 1956.

D. H. LAWRENCE: *Complete Poems*, Heinemann, 1964.
　　　　　　　　Selected Literary Criticism, Heinemann, 1956.

Chapter 5

T. S. ELIOT: *Complete Poems and Plays*, Faber, 1969.
　　　　　Selected Essays, Faber, 1951.
　　　　　On Poetry and Poets, Faber, 1957.
　　　　　To Criticize the Critic, Faber, 1965.
　　　　　The Waste Land: a Facsimile and Transcript, Faber, 1971.

HELEN GARDNER: *The Art of T. S. Eliot*, Cresset Press, 1949.

F. O. MATTHIESSEN: *The Achievement of T. S. Eliot*, Oxford University Press, 1948.

GEORGE WILLIAMSON: *A Reader's Guide to T. S. Eliot*, Thames & Hudson, 1955.

B. C. SOUTHAM: *A Student's Guide to the Selected Poems of T. S. Eliot*, Faber, 1974.

Chapter 6

W. H. AUDEN: *Collected Poems*, Faber, 1976.
　　　　　　The Dyer's Hand, and other essays, Faber, 1963.
　　　　　　Forewords and Afterwords, Faber, 1973.

JOHN FULLER: *A Reader's Guide to W. H. Auden*, Thames & Hudson, 1970.

Chapter 7

LOUIS MACNEICE: *Collected Poems*, Faber, 1966.

WILLIAM T. MCKINNON: *Apollo's Blended Dream: The Poetry of Louis MacNeice*, Oxford, 1971.

D. B. MOORE: *The Poetry of Louis MacNeice*, Leicester University Press, 1972.

JOHN PRESS: *Louis MacNeice*, Longman ('Writers & their Work'), 1965.

C. DAY LEWIS: *Collected Poems*, Chatto & Windus, 1977.

STEPHEN SPENDER: *Collected Poems*, Faber, 1955.
　　　　　　　　The Generous Days, Faber, 1971.

Chapter 8

DYLAN THOMAS: *The Poems*, Dent, 1971.
　　　　　　Under Milk Wood, Dent, 1954.
　　　　　　Portrait of the Artist as a Young Dog, Dent, 1940.
　　　　　　Quite Early One Morning, Dent, 1954.
　　　　　　A Prospect of the Sea, Dent, 1955.
CONSTANTINE FITZGIBBON: *The Life of Dylan Thomas*, Dent, 1965.
PAUL FERRIS: *Dylan Thomas*, Hodder, 1977.
G. S. FRASER: *Dylan Thomas*, Longman ('Writers & their Work'), 1957.

Chapter 9

ROY CAMPBELL: *Collected Poems*, Bodley Head, 3 vols, 1949–60.
GEORGE BARKER: *Collected Poems 1930–55*, Faber, 1957.
　　　　　　The True Confession of George Barker, MacGibbon & Kee, 1965.
DAVID GASCOYNE: *Collected Poems*, Oxford, and Deutsch, 1965.
JOHN BETJEMAN: *Collected Poems*, Murray, 1970 (enlarged edition).
　　　　　　Summoned by Bells, Murray, 1960.
　　　　　　High and Low, Murray, 1967.
　　　　　　A Nip in the Air, Murray, 1974.
STEVIE SMITH: *Collected Poems*, Allen Lane, 1975.
ROY FULLER: *Collected Poems*, Deutsch, 1962.
　　　　　　Buff, Deutsch, 1965.
　　　　　　New Poems, Deutsch, 1968.
　　　　　　Tiny Tears, Deutsch, 1973.
　　　　　　From the Joke Shop, Deutsch, 1975.
GAVIN EWART: *Pleasures of the Flesh*, Ross, 1966.
　　　　　　The Deceptive Grin of the Gravel Porters, Ross, 1968.
　　　　　　The Gavin Ewart Show, Trigram, 1971.
　　　　　　Be My Guest!, Trigram, 1975.
　　　　　　No Fool Like an Old Fool, Gollancz, 1976.
ALUN LEWIS: *Raider's Dawn*, Allen & Unwin, 1942.
　　　　　　Ha! Ha! Among the Trumpets, Allen & Unwin, 1944.
SIDNEY KEYES: *Collected Poems*, Routledge, 1945.
KEITH DOUGLAS: *Collected Poems*, Faber, 1966.
DRUMMOND ALLISON: *The Yellow Night*, Fortune Press, 1944.
CHARLES CAUSLEY: *Collected Poems*, Macmillan, 1975.

Chapter 10

ROBERT GRAVES: *Collected Poems 1975*, Cassell, 1975.
        Goodbye to All That, Cape, 1929.
DOUGLAS DAY: *Swifter than Reason: the Poetry and Criticism of Robert Graves*, Oxford, 1964.
WILLIAM EMPSON: *Collected Poems*, Chatto & Windus, 1955.
ROMA GILL (ed): *William Empson: the Man and His Work*, Routledge, 1974.
EDWIN MUIR: *Collected Poems*, Faber, 1963.
J. C. HALL: *Edwin Muir*, Longman ('Writers & their Work'), 1956.

Chapter 11

PHILIP LARKIN: *The North Ship*, Fortune Press, 1945 (reissued Faber, 1966).
        The Less Deceived, Marvell Press, 1955.
        The Whitsun Weddings, Faber, 1964.
        High Windows, Faber, 1974.
ALAN BROWNJOHN: *Philip Larkin*, Longman ('Writers & their Work'), 1975.
HARRY CHAMBERS (ed): *Phoenix 11/12*, Philip Larkin Issue, 1974.
DAVID TIMMS: *Philip Larkin*, Oliver & Boyd, 1973.
TED HUGHES: *The Hawk in the Rain*, Faber, 1957.
        Lupercal, Faber, 1960.
        Wodwo, Faber, 1967.
        Crow, Faber, 1970 (revised 1972).
        Season Songs, Faber, 1976.
        Gaudete, Faber, 1977.
KEITH SAGAR: *The Art of Ted Hughes*, Cambridge, 1975.

Chapter 12

KINGSLEY AMIS: *A Case of Samples*, Gollancz, 1956.
        A Look Round the Estate, Gollancz, 1967.
EDWIN BROCK: *Song of the Battery Hen: Collected Poems*, Secker & Warburg, 1977.
ALAN BROWNJOHN: *A Song of Good Life*, Secker & Warburg, 1975.
DONALD DAVIE: *Collected Poems 1950–70*, Routledge, 1972.
D. J. ENRIGHT: *Selected Poems*, Chatto & Windus, 1969.
        The Terrible Shears, Chatto & Windus, 1973.
        Sad Ires, Chatto & Windus, 1975.
THOM GUNN: *Poems 1950–66: a Selection*, Faber, 1969.
        Moly, Faber, 1971.
        Jack Straw's Castle, Faber, 1976.

SEAMUS HEANEY: *Death of a Naturalist*, Faber, 1966.
　　　　　　　　Door Into the Dark, Faber, 1969.
　　　　　　　　Wintering Out, Faber, 1973.
　　　　　　　　North, Faber, 1975.
GEOFFREY HILL: *For the Unfallen*, Deutsch, 1959.
　　　　　　　King Log, Deutsch, 1968.
　　　　　　　Mercian Hymns, Deutsch, 1971.
ELIZABETH JENNINGS: *Collected Poems*, Macmillan, 1967.
CHRISTOPHER LOGUE: *Songs*, Hutchinson, 1959.
　　　　　　　　　New Numbers, Cape, 1969.
GEORGE MACBETH: *Collected Poems*, Macmillan, 1971.
ADRIAN MITCHELL: *Out Loud*, Cape, 1968.
　　　　　　　　Ride the Nightmare, Cape, 1971.
PETER PORTER: *The Last of England*, Oxford University Press, 1970.
　　　　　　　Preaching to the Converted, Oxford University Press, 1972.
　　　　　　　Living in a Calm Country, Oxford University Press, 1975.
PETER REDGROVE: *Sons of My Skin: Selected Poems 1954–75*, Routledge, 1975.
R. S. THOMAS: *Selected Poems 1946–68*, Hart Davis MacGibbon, 1974.
　　　　　　Laboratories of the Spirit, Macmillan, 1975.

ANTHOLOGIES

The Faber Book of Modern Verse, edited by Michael Roberts (latest edition revised by Donald Hall), 1965.

Penguin Book of Contemporary Verse, edited by Kenneth Allott, (revised 1962), Penguin.

The Oxford Book of Twentieth Century English Verse, edited by Philip Larkin, Oxford University Press, 1973.

New Lines, edited by Robert Conquest, Macmillan, 1956.

New Lines 2, edited by Robert Conquest, Macmillan, 1963.

The New Poetry, edited by A. Alvarez, Penguin, 1962 (revised 1966).

British Poetry Since 1945, edited by Edward Lucie-Smith, Penguin, 1970.

A Group Anthology, edited by Philip Hobsbaum and Edward Lucie-Smith, Oxford University Press, 1963.

Children of Albion, edited by Michael Horovitz, Penguin, 1969.

Cambridge Book of English Verse 1939–75, edited by Alan Bold, Cambridge, 1976.

Poetry 1900 to 1965, edited by George MacBeth, Longman, 1967.

CRITICISM

The Shaping Spirit (essays on contemporary British and American poets), by A. Alvarez, Chatto & Windus, 1958.

The Survival of Poetry, edited by Martin Dodsworth, Faber, 1970 (includes essays on Gunn, Hughes, Larkin).

The Modern Writer and His World, by G. S. Fraser, Deutsch, and Penguin, 1964.

Vision and Rhetoric: Studies in Modern Poetry, by G. S. Fraser, Faber, 1959.

A Poetry Chronicle: Essays and Reviews, by Ian Hamilton, Faber, 1973.

The Modern Poet: Essays from the Review, edited by Ian Hamilton, Macdonald, 1968.

New Bearings in English Poetry, by F. R. Leavis, Chatto & Windus (revised edition, 1950).

A Map of Modern English Verse, by John Press, Oxford University Press, 1969.

Rule and Energy: Trends in British Poetry since the Second World War, by John Press, Oxford University Press, 1963.

The Society of the Poem, by Jonathan Raban, Harrap, 1971.

Poetry Today 1960–73, by Anthony Thwaite, Longman (for British Council), 1973.

Index

Main references are given in bold type